INVESTOR FACTLINE

INVESTOR FACTLINE:

Finding and Using the Best Investment Information

MICHAEL C. THOMSETT

John Wiley & Sons
New York • Chichester • Brisbane • Toronto • Singapore

Copyright © 1989 by John Wiley & Sons, Inc.

Published by John Wiley & Sons, Inc.

All rights reserved. Published simultaneously in Canada.

Reproduction or translation of any part of this work
beyond that permitted by Section 107 or 108 of the
1976 United States Copyright Act without the permission
of the copyright owner is unlawful. Requests for
permission or further information should be addressed to
the Permissions Department, John Wiley & Sons, Inc.

This publication is designed to provide accurate and
authoritative information in regard to the subject
matter covered. It is sold with the understanding that
the publisher is not engaged in rendering legal, accounting,
or other professional service. If legal advice or other
expert assistance is required, the services of a competent
professional person should be sought. *From a Declaration
of Principles jointly adopted by a Committee of the
American Bar Association and a Committee of Publishers.*

Library of Congress Cataloging-in-Publication Data:
Thomsett, Michael C.
    Investor Factline : Fing and Using the best investment
information / by Michael C. Thomsett.
      p. cm.
    Bibliography: p.
    Includes index.
    ISBN 0-471-61685-0
    1. Investments—Information services. I. Title.
HG4515.9T48 1989
332.6'78—dc19   88-7793
                                                                                                                         CIP

Printed in the United States of America

10 9 8 7 6 5 4 3 2 1

for Maureen and Steve

CONTENTS

	INTRODUCTION: KNOWLEDGE IS PROFIT	*ix*
1	AN APPROACH TO THE MARKET	*1*
2	FUNDAMENTAL AND TECHNICAL ANALYSIS	*19*
3	INVESTIGATING COMPANIES	*47*
4	THE ANNUAL REPORT	*63*
5	THE PROSPECTUS	*85*
6	INVESTMENT ADVISORY LETTERS	*101*
7	FINANCIAL NEWSPAPERS	*113*
8	SEMINARS AND CLASSES	*125*
9	INVESTMENT CLUBS	*137*
10	BROKERS AND FINANCIAL PLANNERS	*147*
11	HOW TO TRACK YOUR INVESTMENTS	*163*
GLOSSARY		*175*
APPENDIX		*197*
INDEX		*203*

INTRODUCTION
KNOWLEDGE IS PROFIT

There are two times in a man's life when he should not speculate: when he can't afford it, and when he can.

Mark Twain

"Send me a thousand dollars today and you'll triple it within a week."

We have all seen or heard claims like this, offered over the phone by salespeople in boiler rooms, or in direct mail ads. The possibility of making a big killing with little or no work will always appeal to a small segment of the population, but smart investors know that choosing an investment requires research, diligence, and hard work. Reckless speculation is a losing venture.

People who profit consistently in the market read, listen, and seek out knowledge from a variety of sources. The financial newspapers, subscription services, books and magazine articles, annual reports, audited financial statements, information filed with the Securities and Exchange Commission (SEC), and even word of mouth are all valuable sources of information.

The problem, though, is figuring out exactly what information will contribute to an informed decision. If you have read financial papers, magazines, or newsletters, or have used a brokerage house's research department, you already know that everyone has a recommendation to make. The difficulty is not in obtaining advice. The dilemma is deciding how to interpret the massive amount of information that is out there and applying it to your own goals and purposes. The first requirement is to define what you expect to achieve with the investments you make.

Nevertheless, the smart approach to investing is based on the gathering of facts. Like any worthwhile endeavor, making money as an investor can be a rewarding personal accomplishment. If you have invested money in the past, you probably appreciate the importance of setting standards and rules you can live by, but you probably are not certain how to put that idea into practice. Well-informed people make smart decisions. It is really a simple formula, but one that few of us are able to follow. The volatility and unpredictability of the stock market make it both exciting and risky. Your success will depend on attaining a level of knowledge that will separate you from the average investor.

The successful investor has abundant information at hand, combined with a healthy dose of common sense. In spite of the jargon and magic formulas, investing really is not as complex as it seems at first glance. If you adopt the attitude that knowledge is profit and pursue your investments with a complete understanding of what you expect to gain, you will be among that minority of people who do succeed and who profit from their best efforts.

INVESTOR FACTLINE

1

AN APPROACH TO THE MARKET

There was a time when a fool and his money were soon parted, but now it happens to everybody.

Adlai Stevenson

How do most people invest? Typically, they start with a call from a broker recommending a stock, or from a salesperson with a mutual fund idea "you won't want to miss."

Investments are sold with the idea that you will make a profit within a reasonable period of time. Claims are made about past performance and the potential for future gains. You have probably heard these claims already:

This mutual fund earned more than any other fund last year.

This stock should rise in value over the next six months.

This is a very strong company, and we're recommending it right now.

Investors who bought shares six months ago have already gained more than 20 percent.

All of these arguments have two common flaws: They are not addressed specifically to you but to investors in general, and they may not be true. A mutual fund that did well in the past will not necessarily perform equally well in the future. And, yes, a stock could rise during the next six months, but it could also fall. How far? How quickly? A company may be described as strong, but what does that mean to you? And if investors who bought shares six months ago made money, how do you know you will, too? Perhaps all the profit has already been made, and now it's too late.

These points raise a lot of questions, and all too often a salesperson does not have the right answers. It will be up to you to define exactly what makes an investment decision a good one for you—right now, next week, or next year.

This book describes an approach to investing that requires definition of your personal goals and risk standards combined with the selective gathering and evaluation of facts. These principles apply to all forms of investment. However, emphasis is on applying them to the stock market, mutual funds, and limited partnerships, because these markets account for the largest portion of investment activity among individuals. The stock market, for example, is highly visible; most daily papers carry news and information about it, including partial or complete listings of activity. Mutual fund popularity has been on the rise since the mid-1970s, and the volume of investment dollars going into funds continues to grow. And for investors seeking diversification into real estate, equipment leasing, and other projects, public limited partnerships—even after the 1986 Tax Reform Act—are very active.

A FIVE-STEP APPROACH

The enlightened approach contains five steps:

1. Define Your Own Goals

The smart investor makes decisions only after correctly determining his personal investing goals. An inexperienced investor may believe that "making a profit" is his goal, and stockbrokers often exploit that simplistic point of view. But profit is not a goal at all but rather a result—the investment results in a profit, usually in the immediate future. A goal is more personal, relating to your own definition of acceptable risk, the purpose of the investment, and your reasons for putting money into investments.

Certainly, you have heard this reasoning before. But what does it really mean? How do you apply it when a broker makes a recommendation? Actually, even investors who are aware of their own goals often do not connect them to actual investment decisions.

A goal is based on your purpose in making investments. For example, are you saving money to buy a house? to put your children through college? for retirement? to start your own business? or simply to save money as a reserve for emergencies? Depending on the purpose, how much risk is appropriate and acceptable? And what forms of risk must be considered when selecting an investment?

In order to develop your goals, you must first evaluate your financial status, level of knowledge, and expectations about available future cash. Also, married couples who will invest together must be certain that they agree on definitions before developing their joint investment goals.

Try this exercise. You and your spouse should answer the following questions without consulting each other. Then compare your answers.

1. Do you consider yourself to be a conservative, a moderate, or a speculator?
2. Will you need the money you invest today in five years, ten years, or beyond?
3. How many years do you consider as short term?
4. How many years do you consider as long term?

You will probably discover that you and your spouse have answered one or more of these questions differently. Yet, the meaning of terms is a basic starting point on which you must agree before you can begin to identify suitable goals together.

If your goals conflict with your spouse's, it will be necessary to compromise, or to structure your financial program so that the goals of both can be met. Then you will need to identify the priorities in your future. That is a matter of discussing the alternatives and placing them in the proper order. Don't be concerned at this point with the financial difficulties in reaching a goal. Simply state what you would like to achieve. The money and the timing come later.

Example: One couple wants to eventually start their own business. They both work and must pay a substantial portion of their income toward their home mortgage. They agree that they will not be able to break away and start their business until the mortgage has been eliminated (or until their savings and income are substantially higher, so that the mortgage represents a smaller percentage of their monthly debt).

Their plan is to prepay the mortgage in 15 years rather than the scheduled 30. Then, with no mortgage on their home, they will be able to start their new business. At the same time, they plan to put some money away for emergencies and invest some money in a mutual fund.

The couple's ultimate goal is to become independent by starting a family business. In order to reach that goal, they develop a plan that eliminates a debt, creates a savings and emergency reserve, and gives them a tangible deadline.

You should invest your money in a market that suits both your goal and your own risk standards. This is where the research comes in, since an investment product will be appropriate only if it matches your goal. For example, if you are trying to build a cash reserve, you should not place your money where you cannot get it back conveniently and promptly; if you plan to buy a house in five years, you do not want your cash tied up for 10 years or more. And if you want to protect your home equity and enjoy the personal security of ownership, you will not be willing to borrow money based on that equity and thus put it at risk.

2. Set Standards for Investing

Never overlook the direct relationship between risk and yield. The greater the potential for fast profits, the greater your risk.

A high-yielding investment that can double within a few days or weeks can drop just as quickly. In comparison, a very conservative investment may yield poorly but present little risk.

Set standards for yourself. Decide how much risk is acceptable to you and how much yield you expect. For example, if you will need access to your money on short notice, look for highly liquid investments like demand savings accounts or money market funds. Or, if you are more interested in accumulating funds for college or retirement, consider growth mutual funds and reinvest all earnings.

Once you understand your goals and have set your own investing standards, you are ready to look for viable investments. Having defined your financial priorities, you will be far ahead of most investors.

3. Check Alternatives

What investments are appropriate to your goals and standards? What a stockbroker may describe as an opportunity may, in fact, be completely wrong for you.

Gather all the information you can. If you have read through any financial magazine or newspaper, you already know that scores of companies offer a free brochure or prospectus. Send away for everything being offered, get your name on all the lists, and subscribe to a market research newsletter. But remember that your final decisions must come, not from the attractive offer itself, but from the definition *you* make of your own investing goals.

4. Research Thoroughly

Getting information is easy, but interpreting it is where the problems begin. You will hear about many stocks, mutual funds, and other investments that sound ideal for you. How do you select the best ones?

Making the right decision depends, without exception, on information. It is not unusual for investors to see the value of their investments fall due to circumstances that were well known or that were actually disclosed in the prospectus. The investors did not take the time to discover those circumstances.

5. Take Action

Once you have completed your research and eliminated the inappropriate investments, you will be left with a few good choices. At that point, invest. You could research excessively and miss a standing opportunity, so it's important to recognize the point at which you have done enough to make an informed decision. You will never eliminate risk completely. It is there to a degree in every investment. Identify a level of risk that is acceptable to you.

Achieving a balance between investigation and action becomes easier with practice. Certainly, you have heard the standard sales pitch, "The opportunity will be gone tomorrow." That is never true. Good investment opportunities can only be dis-

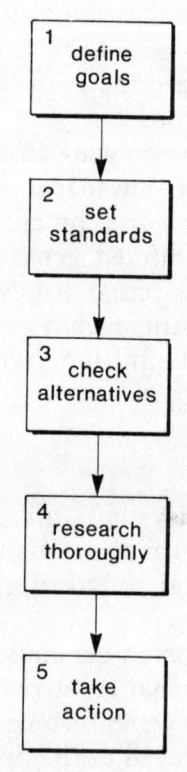

```
┌─────────────┐
│ 1           │
│   define    │
│   goals     │
└──────┬──────┘
       ▼
┌─────────────┐
│ 2           │
│    set      │
│  standards  │
└──────┬──────┘
       ▼
┌─────────────┐
│ 3           │
│   check     │
│ alternatives│
└──────┬──────┘
       ▼
┌─────────────┐
│ 4           │
│  research   │
│ thoroughly  │
└──────┬──────┘
       ▼
┌─────────────┐
│ 5           │
│   take      │
│   action    │
└─────────────┘
```

Figure 1-1. Your Investment Decision

covered with thorough research and action at the right moment. Even so, you could spend the rest of your life researching and never come to the point of decision. Your real experience as an investor comes on the front line, after you have committed money and can see what happens to it.

The five-step approach (Figure 1-1) is not a foolproof method. Every investor makes mistakes. Nevertheless, you will discover that thorough research enables you to come out far ahead of the market on average.

GROUND RULES FOR RESEARCH

All of us have our own "comfort zone" as investors, even though we may not be aware of its limits. Some levels of risk are acceptable; others are not. We also have a minimum requirement for the safety of our investments. Since there is a corresponding relationship between risk and yield, you must be aware of your comfort zone limits before trying to research investments.

Good research can be carried out only if we know what we seek. Eliminating inappropriate investment choices is not only a logical step in the process of investigation; it also saves time and effort. You cannot thoroughly research everything that's available; so your time is better spent looking into those investments most likely to meet your standards.

If you assign an arbitrary scale to every investment and apply your standards as a measure of risk and yield, you can narrow your field of research considerably. For example, on a scale of 1 to 10, 1 is the least risky and lowest-yielding investment, and 10 is the most risky and potentially the highest yielding. This idea is illustrated in Figure 1-2.

For most people, the comfort zone—the place where they can gain an acceptable yield in exchange for an acceptable level of risk—will not be found at the ends of the scale. Overly conservative investments (1s) will yield little or nothing and allow inflation and taxes to erode the buying power of your money. The highly speculative forms of investment (10s) are simply too risky for most of us. So what is acceptable to you is somewhere in the middle. Now it's a matter of defining acceptability.

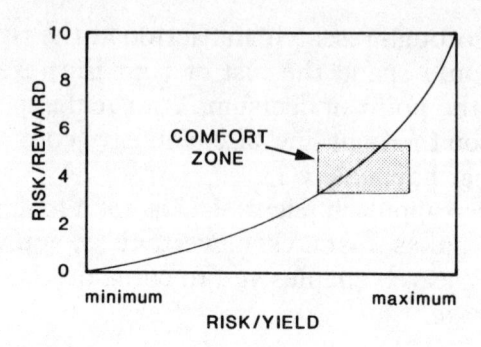

Figure 1-2. The Risk/Yield Curve

To do that, we must discuss the different forms of risk. Most people think of risk as a decline in market value: You buy a stock for $56 per share, risking that it will decline to $30, $25, or lower. But this is only one form of risk. Understanding all forms of risk is the best way to develop your investing standards.

Risk is usually thought of only in terms of profit or loss: There's the chance that your stock's value will rise, but there's also the *risk* that it will fall. But beyond this well-understood market risk, investors face a variety of other dangers. Risk must be defined in a broader context.

There are two main categories into which all forms of risk fall. First is the known event whose timing is uncertain. For example, death is a certainty, but we cannot know when it will occur. Life insurance is a form of protection against this risk; it protects against financial hardship that results from the premature or unexpected death of a family's income earner. The risk is an economic one, since your family is dependent upon your income in order to pay its debts, keep the house, buy clothing, and pay for the children's education.

The second category of risk is an event that might occur, but probably will not. If it does occur, however, it might be catastrophic. Homeowners insurance protects you against the risk of losing your home and its equity, as well as all of your personal belongings. In the event of a fire, your insurance will repay the loss. In all likelihood your home will not burn down, but you cannot afford to take a chance. Your premium and the premiums paid by thousands of others are used to repay the small number of losses that do occur.

The same forms of risk apply to you as an investor. Before deciding where to invest your money, you must understand the types of risk you will assume. Some of those risks are certain events—a profit will, in most cases, be subject to income taxes. Other types of risk are less certain. For example, you might put your money in a highly speculative product in the hope of making a big profit quickly, but in doing so, you accept the risk that you could lose it all.

Several forms of risk must be considered, and you must determine how much risk is acceptable. By going through this exercise, you will strengthen your definition of acceptable investments and will be able to avoid risks you simply cannot tolerate. The various forms of risk to keep in mind include:

1. *Substantial losses in one investment*

The risk in this case arises because an investor puts all available funds into one product. Say an investor has $12,000 and uses it to buy shares of a single stock. That stock then falls in value, even though the market as a whole is on the rise, and the investor loses money.

The way to reduce this risk is through diversification. If you have too little money to achieve a risk spreading among several investments, the best way to diversify is through mutual funds or other pooled investments. A fund can spread its money throughout the market, while individuals often cannot afford to do so.

2. *Illiquidity*

Lack of cash is a severe form of risk. If you commit your money to an investment and cannot get it back, and if you will need funds in the near future, you will suffer a loss. Or, if you go into debt to invest, you must have enough cash to make repayments on your loan each month. If the investment does not yield income, you will have a cash flow problem.

Some types of investment, like limited partnerships or time

deposits, require you to leave money on deposit for many years. You might have to pay a penalty for early withdrawal, or you might even discover that there's no buyer for the shares or units you no longer want. Most limited partnerships, for example, will *not* buy back units from investors who want out; you're expected to tie up your money for 10 years or more. If you will need funds before a liquidation date and you put money into an illiquid investment, you accept a form of risk.

Illiquid investments should be made only with a portion of your total capital, and only when you are certain you can afford to tie up your money for a specified time. That reduces or at least isolates this form of risk.

3. Inflation

All investors must be aware of the need to keep pace with inflation. As prices rise, the buying power of the dollar deteriorates.

Example: You have invested your money in a very conservative, insured account paying a guaranteed rate of 4 percent. However, the rate of inflation over a 10-year period averages 6 percent per year. In this case, you risk losing buying power, since your invested money is worth less on an after-inflation basis.

For investors concerned about inflation, the traditional hedge has been precious metals, which tend to rise in value during inflationary times. However, only part of a total portfolio should be committed to precious metals and other tangible investments. The principle of diversification must be applied here as well.

4. Tax risk

Investors face the risk that profits will be reduced by tax liabilities. A substantial profit will not only be taxable but will also raise the tax bracket for all income earned during the same year. And there are other forms of tax risk to keep in mind. An investment designed to shelter income from taxes could have its status challenged by the IRS, in which case all of your deductions could be disallowed. Thus, you end up with a tax liability rather than a tax write-off, as well as interest and penalties.

To many investors, the ultimate tax risk is being audited.

Some investment products could lead to an audit, particularly if they create unusually high deductions of a questionable nature.

The Tax Reform Act of 1986 tightened the rules for deductibility of passive losses (losses in partnerships and other investments over which you do not exercise direct control), and investment costs now have a ceiling on deductibility. Also, with some forms of favorable tax treatment, you could be liable for the alternative minimum tax.

Tax risks must be accepted or avoided. Too often, investors are taken by surprise when informed that their losses are limited or disallowed. Before investing, you should consult with a tax attorney or accountant, especially if you invest in complex partnerships or tax-free products.

5. *Insurance risk*

There is some risk with all uninsured investments. If you put all of your money into insured accounts, such as savings in a federally insured bank or savings and loan, you eliminate this risk, but you have to accept lower yields than you could get elsewhere.

Stock market investments are not insured; so you risk losing all or part of your money. If the company whose stock you purchase goes out of business, you will suffer from this risk. The solution is to place some of your funds in an insured account and some in a product whose risk is minimal. A mutual fund, for example, buys shares in many companies; so the risk of loss from lack of insurance is diminished by being thinly spread. You can also buy shares in companies whose substantial financial strength reduces the likelihood of a big decline in value.

6. *Excessive leverage*

Leverage is the use of borrowed money to increase your investment basis. For example, an investor has $80,000 available. He can buy a small apartment building for cash, rent it out, and earn a modest return with some cash flow. Enough money comes in from rents each month to cover all expenses, and there is even some left over. In this case, a vacancy would not be cause for alarm, since there's no debt on the property.

The same investor could put $20,000 down on a larger apartment building or on four separate properties, borrowing 80 percent of the total purchase price. With leverage, the investor increases his rental income and gains substantially in the event that market values rise. However, there is also a significant risk: In the event of a high level of vacancies, he might be unable to afford his mortgage payments.

To avoid or reduce leverage risks, you must have enough financial strength to continue debt repayments even when the investment does not produce enough cash flow. Or, you may decide the risk is worth taking and that maximum leverage is the best way to invest. There is no fault in making this decision as long as you understand that your risk is increased as a result.

There is great confusion between risks and goals. Many investment advisers describe the different forms of risk as goals and make statements like, "Your goal should be high liquidity, diversification, and insurance." In fact, these are not goals at all but attributes of specific investment products. A goal is your own reason for investing, and you define an acceptable investment choice in terms of risk factors and safety.

Strengthen your own standards by deciding what is an acceptable level of risk by each type of risk. Then apply this limit to any investment product you are considering buying.

Example: One investor wants to save money for his child's college education. His son is eight, so he will need to build a fund during the next ten years. He is aware of the need for diversification, but he also believes that real estate is the best place to put his money. He is concerned about both inflation and taxes, but is willing to invest without insurance. Most of all, he is concerned with the long-term nature of real estate because he needs to get his money back within the next 10 years.

The solution, he determines, is to buy shares in a Real Estate Investment Trust (REIT). This will answer all of his concerns and fits his risk standards:

1. Diversification

The REIT is diversified. It invests the pooled money it receives in several large real estate developments—a level of diversification that could not be achieved by the investor on his own. The investor also puts money into a savings account each month and owns shares of a mutual fund. Both of these further diversify his portfolio.

2. Liquidity

Many REIT programs are designed for liquidation by a specified date in the future (These are called finite-life REITs)—often 10 years from the inception date. In addition, shares can be bought and sold on the public exchanges, just like corporate stock. Thus, if the investor needs to get his money out before the 10 years have expired, he can place a sell order with his broker.

3. Inflation

The investor believes that real estate is an excellent hedge against inflation. So buying REIT shares fits his standards.

4. Tax risk

REIT programs, compared with other investments, are fairly straightforward. The REIT must pass through profits to investors each year, and these profits are taxed. There is no claim to tax shelter or other favorable treatment and little chance that the IRS will question income or deductions claimed.

5. Insurance risk

The investor is willing to live with the lack of insurance because of the solid historical performance of real estate. And the program's management is experienced in real estate, having many past successes with similar programs. From the investor's point of view, these factors offset the lack of insurance.

6. Leverage

The REIT the investor chose invests strictly in cash and does not borrow money to buy additional properties. Thus, high vacancies would reduce profits but would not threaten the solvency of the entire program.

THE IMPORTANCE OF RESEARCH

Many people understand risk all too well from a past bad experience. If you invested in real estate a few years ago and lost money, you might be determined never to buy real estate again. You may be right, but it is worthwhile keeping an open mind and considering that many forms of investing may meet your standards for safety. If the real estate you purchased was offered through an abusive tax shelter, you probably lost all your money *and* had tax deductions disallowed. That does not mean that real estate is a bad or risky investment, only that the structure of that program was not right for you.

A past negative experience can be used positively to strengthen your research into alternatives. Don't make the mistake of rejecting an investment just because you lost money once before. Instead, use the experience to improve your decision making this time. Take these steps:

1. Evaluate the selection process you used in the past. Where did you make your mistake? Chances are, you selected the investment without defining you own standards and without understanding the degree or type of risk involved.
2. Review a similar investment with today's risk standards and goals in mind. Is there a way that the same type of investment could work for you now?

Example: You once invested in bonds and suffered a loss. You realize now that you were unaware of the significant effect of changing interest rates and did not even consider the financial strength of the corporation issuing the bond. Today, you know you must diversify if you buy bonds again. The solution might be to buy shares in a bond fund.

Many people hear the word "options" and are immediately scared off. They think options are too risky. But there are ways to use the option market that are highly conservative. Options can work as a form of insurance, protecting the value of stocks in your portfolio against declines in value. They can also discount the purchase price of stock with very little risk. Nevertheless, becoming involved in this market requires knowledge and research. Like all forms of investment, the more you know, the better you understand where, if at all, a particular product fits in your overall plan.

There are plenty of salespeople ready to give you advice, hoping you will take the easy way to investing and make a quick decision. But advice that is not based on your personal standards will not make you a success in the market.

Many stockbrokers solicit business on the telephone. How should you respond if you receive a call? First of all, anyone who solicits new business by telephone is probably the least experienced member of a firm—successful brokers are kept too busy by their clients to make cold calls. So you are dealing with someone who has little or no experience. Your response should be "No, thank you," not only because the caller is just starting out, but because he knows nothing about your own risk/yield standards yet is recommending that you buy. That is simply not the way to invest.

You can certainly look into a stock that a caller recommends if you think it might fit into your plan. You can send away for an annual report, filings with the SEC, or copies of research reports. But no decision should be made until you have investigated thoroughly. That's the essence of smart investing —gaining knowledge and then applying what you learn against a well-defined and well-understood standard.

When you take that approach, you reduce all forms of risk. Why? Because your own standard takes risk into account. So the investment alternatives you seriously consider already have attributes you find desirable. And it simplifies your life: If a particular investment is obviously outside your comfort zone, you don't need to waste valuable time researching it.

MAKING THE MATCH

It is that concept of matching—fitting investments into your comfort zone—that is mysterious to the majority of investors. Not understanding the value of research is only part of the problem; most people simply don't know what kinds of investments are right for them.

Research actually begins with self-examination. By going through the process of defining your goals and standards, you have simplified the process of selection. Start your definition by placing every potential investment into one of three classifications:

1. **It fits.** The next step is to research the current status and determine whether the timing is right and if that investment should be made.
2. **It doesn't fit.** You don't need to waste your time looking into it or arguing with a salesperson.
3. **You're not sure.** You need to find out more about the investment and its inherent risks. Every investment has specific characteristics that define risk in every respect. Those are the points you need to discover before deciding whether the investment fits your standards.

Successful investors share certain characteristics in their approach to investing. First, they understand exactly what kind of investor they are. There's no doubt about where they stand. Second, they have specific goals, which they probably use on several levels. (They know why they're investing, and they know when to buy and sell with a specific target in mind.) Third, they follow the rules they set for themselves. Many investors fail because they don't understand the importance of this idea.

Example: An investor buys shares of stock for $27 per share. His rule is that he will sell if the stock rises to $33 or higher per share, or if it falls to $24 or lower. This is a good approach because it sets an income goal and defines the limit of acceptable loss. But can he follow his own rules?

At one point, the stock rises rapidly to $34 per share, but, in spite of his rule, he delays selling, fearing he will lose out if the stock continues to climb. Then it begins falling, finally settling at $22. Still, he doesn't sell. He thinks, "I have to get back at least to my purchase price." You can probably predict what will happen if the stock does rise to the original value of $27 per share. He will hold on, hoping for yet more profit. In reality, no profit is earned until the stock is sold, but investors tend to count paper profits as real and earned—an error in thinking.

In a situation like that, you can't possibly win. You break your own rules whether the stock goes up or down in value. It makes much more sense to buy on the basis of solid research, within the definition of what is acceptable, and with exact rules. Then, if you reach a price limit—up or down—you sell. People who follow their rules will make a profit in the market and will cut their losses when the value of their investments falls.

2

FUNDAMENTAL AND TECHNICAL ANALYSIS

*If you can look into the seeds of time,
And say which grains will grow and which will not,
Speak then to me.*

William Shakespeare

In any discussion of investing, arguments for past trends are inevitable; yet the past has proven to be a poor indicator of future performance. So why the emphasis on the past? Because if you want to succeed as an investor, you soon discover that an educated guess is better than just a simple guess.

This is especially true in the stock market, where it is not value, but the *perception* of value, that determines price movement of stocks. The study of financial facts or trends can be useful in reaching a decision, but you must still make that decision based on your own risk standards.

There is no crime in turning to the past and analyzing the information found there. And there is nothing wrong with using the results of your analysis to improve your guesswork. The danger in analysis occurs when someone claims to offer you a certain formula that actually does not work. You will benefit from analysis by thinking of it as one of several sources of information available to you, to be used as a test of a stock against your well-defined comfort zone.

FORMS OF ANALYSIS

There are two general kinds of analysis: fundamental and technical. They can be used either alone or in combination to gather information on possible investments. But don't fall into the trap of closing your mind because one limited formula promises an inside track to the "right" answer.

Fundamental analysis—also called quantitative analysis—is a study of the numbers and of tangible information on profits, products and services, and financial strength. It could be thought of as the accounting approach to investing. In companies, accountants predict future profits, costs, and expenses on the basis of what has happened in the recent past. In that situation, the future is controllable because management has the opportunity to create markets, reduce costs, and build profits.

In the market, however, there is a basic problem in depending only on fundamental analysis. You can compare the financial strength of numerous companies and track profits, dividends, upcoming product developments, and financial ratios before deciding to buy the stock of the one that seems strongest. The problem is that your analysis is no guarantee that the stock's value will rise in the future.

This is a reality of the market: Value is set not by fundamental strength, but by the collective perception of investors about the *future* value of that company.

Example: The analysts predict that one company's quarterly earnings will rise by 15 percent in the coming quarter. However, when results are posted, profits have risen by only 10 percent. On the day of the announcement, the stock's value drops five points.

The general assumption is that the prediction of future earnings has been factored into the current price of the stock. But because actual profits are lower than what the analysts said they would be, it's bad news. The 15 percent projection was factored into the current price, but only 10 percent was realized. And it does not matter that the company's earnings have been consistently strong, that profits are on the rise, and that the company is the leader in its industry. Simply put, the fundamentals don't always apply and cannot be used in isolation to pick sure winners.

Technical analysis—also called qualitative analysis—is the study of pure trends, in which the making and timing of decisions are based not on financial facts but on price patterns, volume, performance, or the application of mathematical formulae.

Technicians believe that stocks, industries, and the market as a whole establish patterns and operate within cycles, and that those patterns and cycles are predictable. The most popular form of technical analysis is charting—the study of price movements to time buy and sell decisions.

Technical analysis, by itself, ignores the financial realities that affect price and investor perceptions. For example, a computer company releases a new line of hardware that is cheaper, more efficient and dependable, and smaller than that offered by the competition. The consensus of opinion is that this new line will be highly successful. Advance orders are high, and the product is an immediate success. A fundamentalist sees this as a positive sign for the future value of stock, but a technician, studying the trading pattern, may conclude the opposite.

Fundamental and technical analysis can be useful if used together and as only one part of your analysis. Both techniques have flaws, though, that make them less than dependable as the sole methods for picking stocks. The unpredictability of the future cannot be reduced to formulae, nor can anyone consistently and accurately claim that signals in the present or past always show the way. So many future events—some outside the market itself—can affect value, that any exclusive formula for investing is bound to be flawed.

Moreover, since any publicly available information must be presumed to be in the hands of all other investors, the conclusions you draw about how that information *should* affect a stock's value will already be reflected in the price of the stock. This is the "efficient market theory"—a belief that the changes in a stock's price allow for all known factors. If this theory is accurate, it raises a serious question: If the price has already changed because of fundamental information, what good does it do to perform your own analysis?

This point is emphasized in the book, *The Random Walk*

and Beyond, by Mark A. Johnson (John Wiley & Sons, 1988). Johnson reports on a number of studies of the market over a span of years. He states:

> If the stock market is efficient, then investment skill is inconsequential, because all stocks are fairly valued. Nevertheless, even if they are all fairly valued and equally viable investment candidates, they certainly will not all turn out equally well. Unpredictable future developments will affect the performance of each stock, and results will vary widely. In an efficient market, we may not be rewarded for our skill; we will be rewarded—or punished—for our luck.[1]

One of the factors that cloud our judgment as investors is the degree to which analysts will go to prove their case. The real competition in the market, it often seems, is not between companies but between analysts—with all claiming their method is better than anyone else's. Johnson comments on this reality:

> Investing seems highly complex, but once we cut through the jargon, the fancy mathematical models, the intimidation, the hype, and the cult of expertise, we find a surprisingly simple and logical situation. Our challenge is to let go of traditional and habitual modes of thought and habit. Most investors who are losing in the stock market are not stupid; they are just playing the wrong game. As a serious investor, I dare you *not* to match wits with Wall Street.[2]

FUNDAMENTAL ANALYSIS

A study of the past numbers and an estimate of what the future holds, by themselves, cannot point to the best investment. However, such information is of great value as long as you understand

---

1. Mark A. Johnson, *The Random Walk and Beyond: An Inside Guide to the Stock Market* (New York: John Wiley & Sons, Inc., 1988), p. 60. Reprinted by permission of the publisher.

2. Johnson, *The Random Walk and Beyond*, p. 8. Reprinted by permission of the publisher.

its limitations. For example, in a comparison of two different companies, one shows a history of increases in dividends, sales, profits, and other measures of financial strength. The other shows a very inconsistent history: Two years of modest profits are followed by a year of huge losses; dividends are increased, decreased, or even missed in some years; and the ratio of borrowed money to equity varies from one year to the next.

A conservative investor will recognize at once that the second company is struggling and has been unable to establish firm control over its financial life. Chances are, its results vary according to competitive pressures, style and quality of management, and many other factors. Whatever you conclude from a study of fundamentals, this information itself is most helpful, if not in identifying a good investment candidate, then at least in eliminating some companies from your search.

The fundamentals should be examined as part of a trend, not in isolation. For example, the one-page summaries sent to subscribers of the "Value Line Investment Survey" show several years of basic fundamental information, which will be useful to your evaluation. A typical four-year summary of some key fundamentals might look like that shown in the table below. (For more detailed information on Value Line and other research services, refer to Chapter 3, "Investigating Companies.")

Any report of financial results, predictions, and other facts or estimates related to value can be considered a form of fun-

Fundamental Analysis

	1985	1986	1987	1988
Dividends per share	.15	.16	.16	.17
Earnings per share	.94	1.17	1.36	1.15
Book value per share	8.03	9.15	12.30	12.51
Average P/E ratio	16.1	15.1	11.1	10.0
Annual sales (millions of dollars)	69.6	67.4	75.3	109.8
Operating margin	11.3%	9.9%	12.8%	12.4%
Net profits (millions of dollars)	1.5	1.4	4.2	5.1

damental analysis. The most common fundamental indicators include:

Financial Statements

A company's balance sheet, income statement, and cash flow summaries report its status and the results of its operations. An analysis of the numbers through comparison and ratios is the most popular and widely used form of fundamental analysis.

Dividends Paid

Dividends are distributions of net profits to shareholders. While the amount per 100 shares might be relatively small—especially in light of potential price appreciation—the importance of dividend trends is substantial.

The dividend income you earn as an investor can represent a significant portion of your total return, a fact that must not be overlooked. However, analysts attach a high degree of importance to the idea that a company should match or increase its dividend each year. Those companies that have done so for many decades point to this fact with pride. Thus, the pressure to pay dividends is great even in a year when results are poor. If skipping a dividend is prudent, you must ask how wise it is to declare a dividend this year.

Some corporations do not pay dividends to their shareholders. They argue that it is better to invest that capital in future growth. Which philosophy is right? It depends on your point of view and opinion. There is no absolute formula for equating dividend payments with financial strength for each company.

To decide how important dividend yield should be to you, you must decide whether you are investing for growth or for income. A growth stock might perform and grow in value if profits are reinvested in future growth rather than paid out as profits to investors. However, if you want current income rather than long-term growth, you should consider stocks that tend to pay high dividends even at the expense of potential price appreciation.

Book Value Per Share

To understand how unrelated the fundamentals are to perceived future value, consider book value per share—the tangible value of stock—which is perhaps the most ignored fundamental indicator.

Book value per share is computed by dividing tangible book value by the number of outstanding common shares. In many instances, book value may be far above or below the current market value of stock. You might be able to buy stock far below its tangible book value, or you may be willing to pay a premium far above it. The point is that book value has little to do with the market's perception of a company's value.

Because book value is the *tangible* value of a company, it can be seen as a safety level. In the worst case, a company would be forced to liquidate all of its assets and pay off all of its debts. Based on today's numbers, the book value per share is the amount you would receive if that happened. So if book value is $25 per share and today's price is $38, you risk only $13 in perceived value. In essence, the market perception is that this company has potential above its tangible value. Investors are willing to pay a premium in the belief that the stock's price will rise, and if they are right, profits will increase both market and book value in the future.

Earnings Per Share

The total net earnings divided by the number of outstanding shares of common stock produces the earnings per share. This ratio is used frequently for comparisons between one year and the next. An increase is positive, but be aware that there is a natural ceiling in the amount of growth you can expect.

The statistics can be deceptive. For example, when a company buys its own shares, retiring a large block of common stock, that action will increase the earnings per outstanding share even when profits are down.

The trend in earnings per share is an excellent fundamental indicator for judging growth over many years. If the earnings have been consistent, that's a sign that management has created controlled, well-planned growth from one year to the next. But if earnings per share are erratic, showing both large increases and occasional losses, then the predictability of that stock's price will be lower and a long-term growth pattern will be more difficult to estimate.

Price/Earnings Ratio

The price/earnings (P/E) ratio is probably the most overrated and misused fundamental indicator. It is determined by dividing the current share price by the earnings per share. The theory behind this ratio is that the larger the P/E, the greater the demand for the stock and the greater the likelihood of future growth.

Remember, though, that the P/E ratio is hindsight; it reflects what has occurred in the past. By the time the P/E ratio has increased, it's too late to benefit from the runup in price. If a stock sold five years ago for 5 times earnings and sells today for 20 times earnings, the price has already increased substantially.

Another disturbing fact about the P/E ratio is that, historically, lower P/E stocks have actually performed better than higher P/E stocks—not the other way around, as is widely believed. That's because the runup has not yet occurred. Johnson reports on these findings in *The Random Walk and Beyond*:

> Studies have confirmed repeatedly that returns *are* related to P/Es. To put the matter succinctly, *low-P/E stocks outperform high-P/E stocks*. When we consider how fundamental and accessible a measure of value the price/earnings ratio is, this finding is a rather severe blow to the efficient market theory.[3]

Other Financial Measures

A number of other factors are analyzed in the fundamental approach. These include trends in gross sales, gross profit margin, net profits, and cash flow.

3. Johnson, *The Random Walk and Beyond*, p. 120. Reprinted by permission of the publisher.

The fundamentalists also watch what occurs off the balance sheet. They measure relative market share within an industry, moves to reduce costs and expenses, the elimination of subsidiaries that have lost money in the past, development of new product lines, the sale of assets, accounting changes, and extraordinary adjustments.

You can be misled by relying too much on fundamental analysis to pick a stock that is likely to rise in value. The best use of this analysis tool is to identify and eliminate candidates that fall outside of your risk selection criteria.

Example: An investor decides that a stock he selects must show historical consistency in earnings per share, that its dividend rate must be 5 percent or more, and that it must have outperformed its industry competitors in gross sales and net profits for three of the last five years.

These criteria are quite specific and will not be met in every industry you want to review. But if you are comparing investment possibilities in five or more different industries, an analysis may well point to a few strong candidates. From there, the selection may be further narrowed down by applying standards and tests beyond the fundamentals.

TECHNICAL ANALYSIS

The purely fundamental analyst considers the technician little more than a witch doctor. And, of course, the technician, believing in patterns and predictability, thinks the fundamentals are completely unrelated to price movement.

To a degree, both sides are right. Neither method is solely dependable, and neither offers enough information for you to make a completely informed decision. Yet most investors depend on technical indicators to some degree, even basing their attitude toward the market on movement in an index.

Technicians believe in the efficient market theory, which holds that, by and large, every *other* investor has already performed fundamental analysis before deciding which stocks to buy, hold, or sell. Thus, all known information is disseminated or discounted in the current market price. Technicians do not care about the quality or source of information; they are concerned with the behavior of stock prices.

The technician respects trends and refuses to believe that price movement is arbitrary. He bases current thinking on an analysis of moving averages combined with volume. (Of course, this is only one of many technical methods, but it is one that is widely used.)

The daily high and low prices of a stock are computed as a moving average. Thus, for any one day, the range of prices will reflect an average over a longer period of time. By combining on one chart the daily trading range and the longer-term trend, the

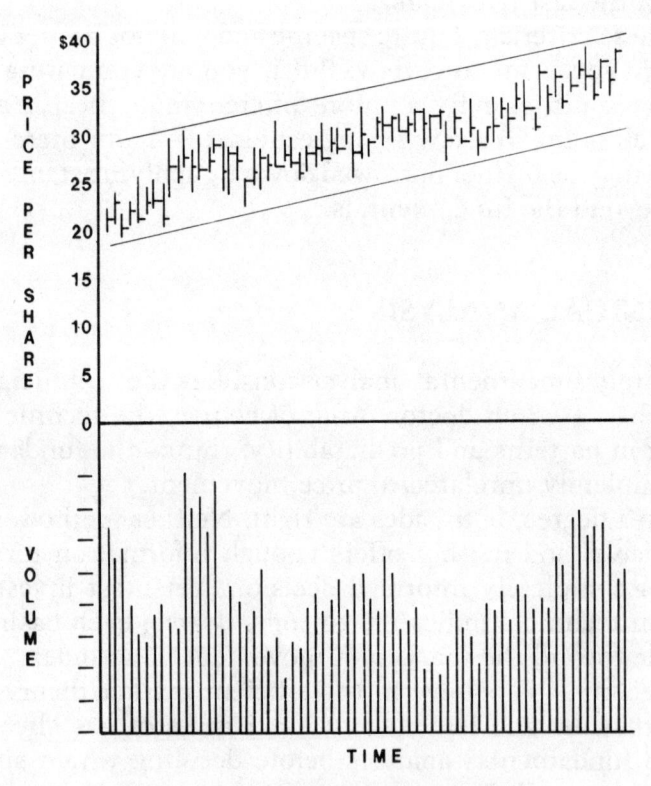

Figure 2-1. The Moving Average

technician believes she can accurately anticipate future price ranges and trends. Changes in the level of trading volume further support the apparent trend, or are seen as a signal that a price movement is about to reverse. The technician believes that price is a reflection of all known fundamental information and that volume is an indicator of demand and market reponse. Thus, any change in volume is seen by the technician as a signal.

A moving average chart is shown in Figure 2-1.

The assumption of market efficiency is expressed in the Dow Theory. This theory holds that market *averages* change in anticipation of value. Thus, future price changes can be anticipated by following the indexes.

The Dow Theory identifies two broad classifications of price movement. Primary movements last from one to five years and establish a general tendency for prices to rise (a bull market) or fall (a bear market). Secondary movements, lasting from one to three months, occur within primary movements and anticipate shifts in them. The primary and secondary movement theory is illustrated in Figure 2-2.

In order for the technical approach to work, you must first believe that price patterns are predictable, and that belief is a questionable one. It assumes a degree of intelligence or logic in

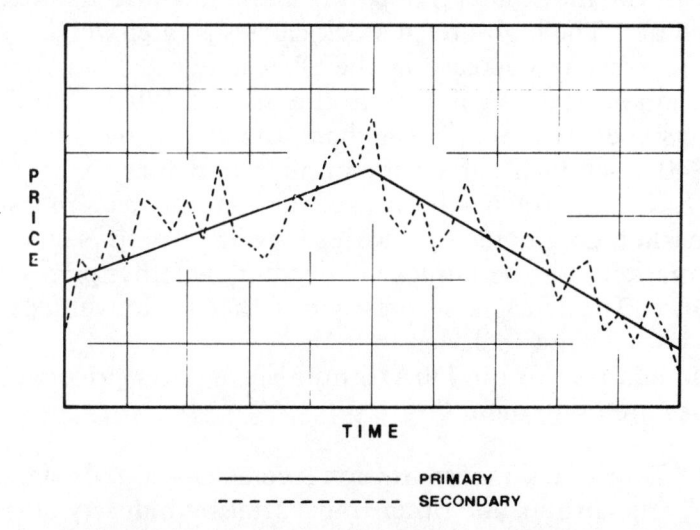

Figure 2-2. Primary and Secondary Movement

the movement of stock prices, which, a study of the fundamentals shows clearly, does not exist.

Remember that it is the perception of future value rather than current and past fact that influences the value of stock. With that in mind, you must expect prices to reflect the ever-changing beliefs of all investors. In reality, price movement usually reflects an overreaction to news, good or bad.

One problem with the belief that current prices reflect all known information is in the way people invest. The reasons for buying a particular stock usually are not based on fundamental information; rather, the decision is the result of faulty assumptions, others' advice, or a preconceived notion about a company's quality or value.

To see the flaw in technical thinking, consider the most widely followed technical index, the Dow Jones Industrial Averages (DJIA). The DJIA is made up of 30 stocks, with each issue's contribution to the average adjusted for stock splits. This index is price-weighted, meaning that higher-priced stocks have more influence on the averages than lower-priced stocks. The per-share price by itself is meaningless, since a stock split results in more shares and a lower price. Thus, price weighting is a form of distortion. For example, what happens when a high-priced stock in the index falls five points and a low-priced stock rises five points? The high-priced stock carries greater weight; so the daily increase or decrease in the DJIA is not necessarily a true reflection of what is going on in the market. When a stock falls from $80 per share to $75 per share, the weighting is twice that of a $40 stock losing the same number of points.

Still, the DJIA has been used consistently as a measure of the market. Originated by Charles Dow in 1884, it is considered "the market" for the purpose of deciding whether prices are up or down. The DJIA is so prestigious that its movement often affects stocks not included in it.

In addition to the DJIA, a number of other price-weighted indexes are used, including:

- ☐ Dow Jones Transportation Averages—20 railroad, trucking, airline, and other transportation industry stocks.
- ☐ Dow Jones Utility Averages—15 major utility stocks.

☐ Dow Jones Composite Averages—all 65 stocks included in the other three indexes.

A more accurate measurement than a price-weighted index is a value-weighted index, such as the Standard & Poor's 500 Index. Started in 1967, Standard & Poor's 500 is actually a composite of four other indexes: 400 industrials, 20 transportation, 40 financial, and 40 public utility stocks. Also value-weighted is the New York Stock Exchange Index, which includes *all* listed common stocks. The movement in daily prices is accurately reflected in this index because it is broad and is not weighted according to price.

Other value-weighted indexes are the National Association of Securities Dealers Automated Quotations—Over-The-Counter (NASDAQ-OTC) Price Index, started in 1971, which includes all NASDAQ-listed common stocks; and the American Stock Exchange Price Change Index, which lists all listed stocks on the American Stock Exchange without price weighting.

A third kind of technical index, and perhaps the most accurate, is the equally weighted index. In this kind, the percentage price movement in each stock is given equal value. Thus, a 5 percent change affects the index on a percentage basis rather than on a proportional price basis. An example of an equally weighted index is one published by Value Line.

TECHNICAL INDICATORS

There are a number of diverse technical indicators in use today, some so offbeat as to be amusing. For example, some people claim they can predict market price movements on the basis of changes in global weather, the outcome of sporting events, or the thickness of tree rings. The more logical technical indicators are at least directly related to something occurring in the market itself.

Many technical analysts subscribe to the contrarian theory. This is a belief that the prevailing sentiment in the market is usually wrong and thus opposite actions should be taken. For example, a contrarian will see a mood of fear as a sign that the market is at a low. If prices have declined to the point where most investors have pulled out of the market, the contrarian recognizes a buy signal. The same is true when enthusiasm runs high. The contrarian sees excessive optimism as a bullish sign and decides it is time to pull out.

Some of the more popular technical indicators are:

Insider Trading

An "insider" is a corporate officer or major shareholder, who is perhaps the best judge of what is occurring in the company. Technicians watch trends in buy and sell orders among corporate insiders. When insider buying activity increases, that is a technical sign that the stock is a worthwhile investment—based on the belief that the insider is in the best position to know. And when insider selling increases, that is a sign that the stock is likely to fall in value in the near future.

Mutual Fund Indicators

When mutual funds have a lot of cash on hand, that is an indication that demand for securities is pending. At some point in the near future, the funds—representing a good portion of total trading volume—will begin buying, and that will drive prices up.

When the funds are fully invested, the technician takes that as a sign that the momentum of demand has topped out and that prices will fall in the near future. Another indicator taken from mutual fund activity is the rate of share redemptions. If it is true that most investors are always wrong, an increase in redemptions signals that the market will be going up in the future.

Mutual fund indicators may be especially useful in the timing of fund buying and selling. If you agree with the contrarian approach, you certainly do not want to buy fund shares when capital is fully invested. And if you own shares at that point, you may want to sell and then repurchase when the fund has a lot of cash on hand.

Many mutual fund investors, seeking long-term growth, deposit the same amount in their accounts each month and reinvest all earnings. Others like to switch and exchange their shares according to the indicators that technicians watch. This is a more speculative approach to fund investing; however, many fund switching services have earned their subscribers returns in excess of 20 percent per year.

Odd-lot Index

Another contrarian point of view assumes that those who buy odd lots—purchases of less than 100 shares—are not smart investors. The belief, called the odd-lot theory, is that these investors invariably buy near the top and sell at the bottom. Thus, an increase in odd-lot buying, to the technician, is a sell signal.

One application of this technical principle is the timing of mutual fund or direct buying and selling of stocks. You may see an increase in odd-lot activity (a sign that less sophisticated investors are entering the market) as a signal to redeem your mutual fund shares or take profits in stocks and wait out the market. Then, as market sentiment declines with price trends, and odd-lot activity is minimal, you can repurchase in expectation of a price increase.

Breadth of the Market

A popular technical index, called the breadth index, measures what is called the breadth of the market. This is represented by the trend in daily advances and declines.

The breadth index is a plus or minus percentage calculated this way: Each day's declines are subtracted from advances and the sum is divided by total issues traded. When declines exceed advances, the smaller number is subtracted from the larger, and the resulting percentage is a negative.

Example: On one day, 912 issues advanced, 701 declined, and 184 remained unchanged (the total involved was 1797). The breadth index is:

$$\frac{912 - 701}{1797} = 11.7\%$$

34   *Investor Factline*

By tracking the advances and declines each day, the technician attempts to predict overall bullish or bearish tendencies. Most financial newspapers issue a summary for the last five days, reporting issues traded, advances, declines, unchanged, new highs, and new lows. For example:

	Friday	*Thursday*	*Wednesday*	*Tuesday*	*Monday*
Issues traded	1,941	1,948	1,976	1,964	1,981
Advances	743	812	618	1,043	1,506
Declines	1,003	916	984	801	312
Unchanged	195	220	374	120	163
New highs	26	11	14	7	19
New lows	11	8	15	3	10

The trend in the advance–decline line can be charted by simply subtracting one from the other and entering the net difference for each day. An advance–decline chart is shown in Figure 2-3.

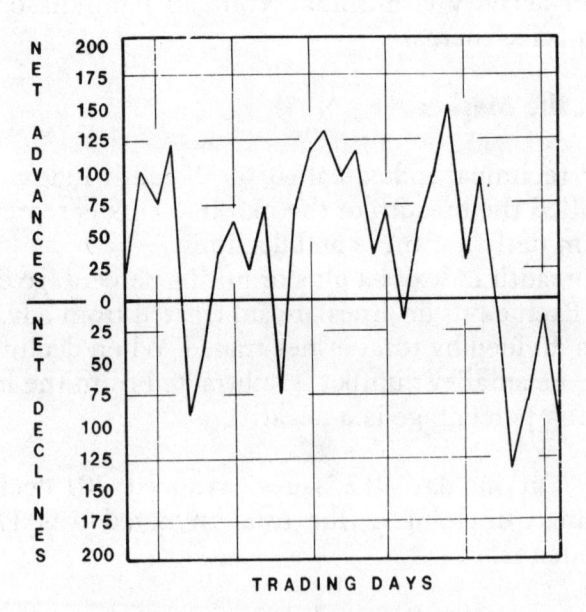

Figure 2-3. Advance-Decline Chart

Short Interest

One technical theory holds that trends in outstanding "short interest" are worth following. Short interest is the amount of open short positions in stock. Short sellers must become buyers at some point in the future to cover their positions; so the contrarian might conclude that a rise in short interest is a buy signal and that a drop is a sell signal, on the assumption that active short sellers will be wrong most of the time.

You watch short interest trends and notice that the level has grown substantially during the last month. As a contrarian, you assume that the investors with short positions are likely to be wrong and see that as a buy signal.

Investor Confidence

The degree of confidence investors have in the near-term future—the confidence index—might also be called the "anxiety" index. The idea is that price movements are based primarily on the level of confidence that investors have in the market. The level of confidence may be measured in several ways. For example, Barron's Confidence Index bases its measurements on trends in the bond market, the theory being that money is invested in either bonds or stocks and that a decrease in one type of investment is accompanied by an increase in the other. Thus, increases or decreases in bond yields are used as the basis for measuring confidence.

Volume

Closely related to the confidence index is the current trend in daily trading volume. High volume during a price upswing is considered bullish, but high volume when prices are falling is thought to be bearish.

Technicians point to the past, with reason. Volume has tended to increase gradually during weakness in the market just before significant drops in price. "Significant" may refer either to a percentage of value drop or to a number of points lost.

Judge the dependability of volume trends by tracking not only overall market price trends but price trends *with* volume level trends. You may recognize increasing volume immediately preceding insignificant price changes and can use that information to better time your own market decisions.

Block Trading

Technicians follow trends in block trading, that is, buy or sell orders for 10,000 or more shares at one time. A major sale in large blocks (indicating high institutional selling) can anticipate pending drops in overall market value.

Block trades are made by institutional investors—mutual funds, pension plans, insurance companies, and other organizations managing large pools of money. Institutions account for the larger portion of capital in the market, but the individual, or "retail," investor's share is increasing, and retail activity accounts for the majority of daily trades.

Institutional activity can affect market prices by sheer volume. When an institution sells off a major holding in one company, for example, the sudden availability of thousands of shares will probably drive the market price down. And when an institution buys up all the shares it can find in a company, that will invariably drive the price up.

You can follow block trading in particular stocks in several ways. If you assume the contrarian view, you believe institutions will time their trades incorrectly. A large sell will reduce the price, meaning a buying opportunity for you. If, however, you believe that institutions have more immediate access to information than you have, you may imitate their buying and selling activity.

New Issues

Technicians predict market sentiment by watching trends in new issues. These trends include the rate of new issues, investor response, and performance during the first few weeks that new issues are on the market. When market sentiment is optimistic, there may be an increase in new issue activity as well as in investor response. The contrarian point of view is that as the level of new issue activity climbs, the signal is increasingly bearish, and it may be time to sell.

Industry Trends

Certain leading industries are watched closely by some technicians. At various times, certain industry groups are thought to lead the market. By anticipating rises and falls in price in these groups, the technician anticipates how the rest of the market will follow.

Many investors time their decisions on the basis of activity in particular industries. They decide when to buy or sell according to price trends not just for one company, but for the industry as a whole. No one industry will always lead the market; it is constantly changing. But by tracking the current leading industry trends, you may predict overall price movements and time decisions accordingly.

Beta

Beta is a way of measuring a stock's volatility against the market as a whole. For example, if the market increases in value by 2 percent, and one particular stock follows at the same percentage, that stock's beta is 1.0. However, if the stock tends to grow at a faster pace, its beta is higher, and if it reacts at a slower pace, its beta is lower. A stock with a beta of 0.8 will, on average, respond to overall market trends by 80 percent.

One way to select stocks suited to your own risk standards is to restrict your candidate list to issues with specific beta records. For example, you may want a stock that responds below the market average in the belief that the market as a whole is too volatile; or, if you are willing to assume a greater degree of risk, you may seek stocks with high beta histories.

Volatility

Volatility is a measure of a stock's tendency to change prices within a given range. It is computed as the percentage of swing in prices during the last year.

Example: One stock's high–low range during the last 12 months was between 35 and 29. To compute volatility, divide the difference by the low:

$$\frac{35 - 29}{29} = 20.7\%$$

Although the price range for two different stocks may be identical, the volatility can be vastly different. In the example above, a 6-point swing resulted in volatility of 20.7 percent. But consider this example:

$$\frac{83 - 77}{77} = 7.8\%$$

This stock is much less volatile because its price range is higher. Volatility should be judged not only by the number of points it moves within a year, but also by the point movement and price range together.

As part of your selection process, consider volatility in line with the degree of risk you are willing to assume. A highly volatile stock should be viewed as a greater risk because chances of a big decline in its prices are greater than for stocks with relatively low volatility records. At the same time, more volatile stocks will benefit the most when the market is on the rise. You must weigh the volatility factor and its risk against the potential for profits and losses. If you make this judgment according to your own standards, you will narrow your list.

CHARTING STOCKS

Chartists are technicians who believe that visible patterns in stock price movement foretell the immediate future, and that stocks establish and then repeat trading patterns.

One quick form used by chartists is the point and figure chart. Each day's trading range is entered on a grid in which each square represents one point in price. The closing price is not

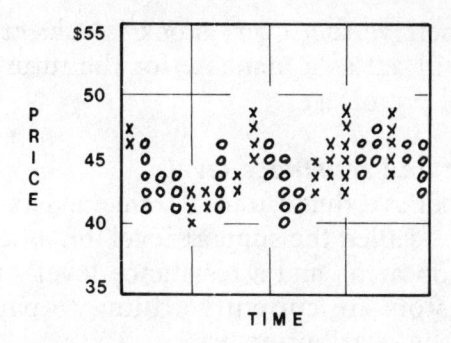

Figure 2-4. Point and Figure Chart

used, only the trading range. An x indicates a rise in price, an o a drop. The point and figure chart is thought not only to show a tendency toward rising or falling prices, but also to give a daily trading range. A typical point and figure chart is shown in Figure 2-4.

Another popular form is the vertical line chart, which uses a symbol for each day's trading range and closing price. A vertical line represents the range from high to low, and a smaller, horizontal line represents the closing price. A typical chart is shown in Figure 2-5.

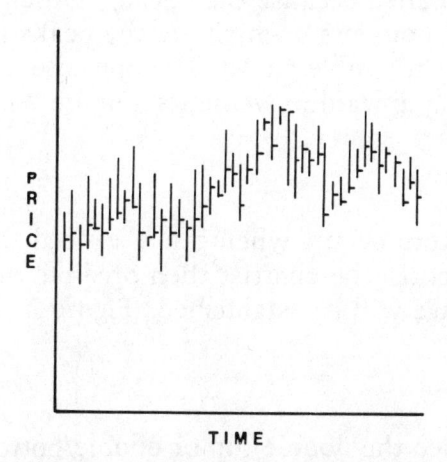

Figure 2-5. Vertical Line Chart

Chartists believe that every stock is subject to trends and that the past will act as a mandate for the future. This theory involves several premises:

1. Support and resistance levels

Chartists believe that a trading range exists between a potential low price, called the support level (or, as a trading range, the accumulation area), and a resistance level—the maximum price that investors are currently willing to pay. The trading range is called the distribution area.

2. Significance of deviation

Chartists claim that when prices move from the predictable trading range dictated by the chart, a major signal is always indicated. The breakaway gap—a space between two days' trading ranges—is considered a signal of pending major movements.

3. Predictability of patterns

Chartists contend that certain patterns foretell price movement. Some of these patterns are described below.

Head and Shoulders

A downward trend is indicated when price movements peak in an *M* shape (so-called because the "head," which is the middle peak, and the "shoulders," which are the peaks to the left and right, somewhat resemble an *M*). The opposite, a *W* shape, anticipates pending upward movements. (Figure 2-6)

Breakout Pattern

A breakout pattern occurs when prices exceed the range of resistance or support. The chartist then predicts that an entirely new trading range will be established. (Figure 2-7)

Double Signals

Chartists also see the double top or double bottom as a signal of upcoming movement. For example, when price movement

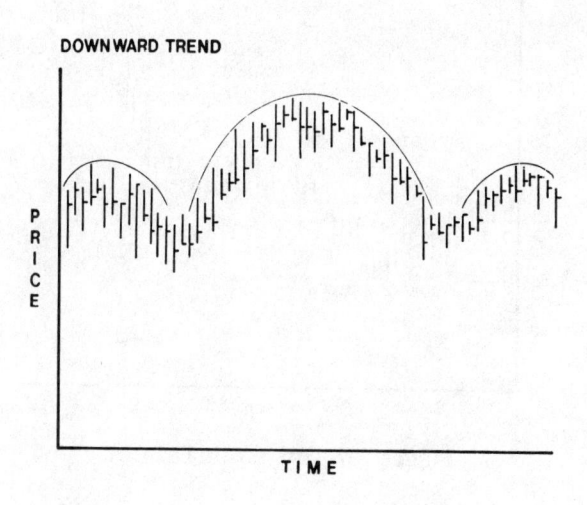

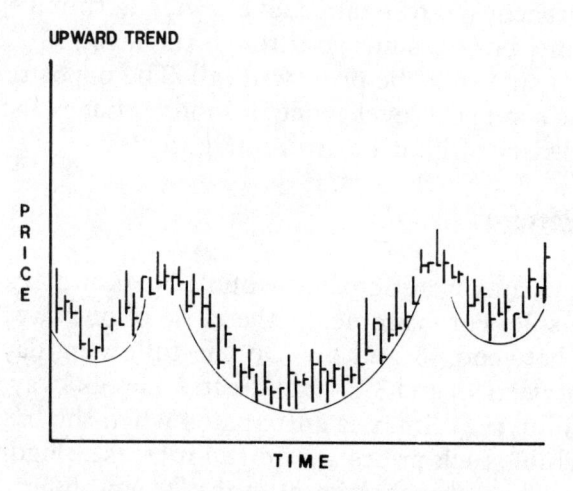

Figure 2-6. Head and Shoulders Pattern

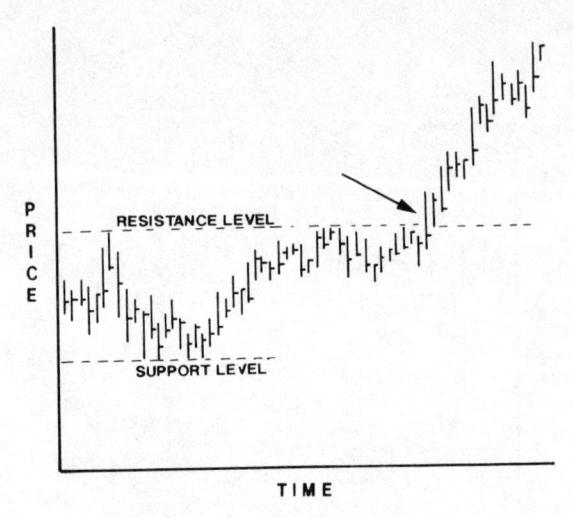

Figure 2-7. Breakout Pattern

tests (approaches) a resistance level twice within a specified period of time, but does not go through the level, it is often interpreted as a sign that the price will fall. The opposite is believed for testing a support level twice or more—that is a sign that the price will rise in the near future. (Figure 2-8)

Climax Patterns

A selling climax is anticipated when a breakaway gap occurs on the downside. For example, at the close of one day, the trading range is between 48 and 46. On the following day, the stock trades between 43 and 39—that creates a breakaway gap of three points. A buying climax is anticipated when the breakaway gap occurs while stock prices are on the increase. (Figure 2-9)

Invariably, the chartist attempts to combine the study of chart patterns with that of other technical signs. These signs include trends in volume as well as many of the other indicators listed in preceding pages—odd-lot, short interest, advance-decline, and so forth.

The use of both fundamental and technical analysis can

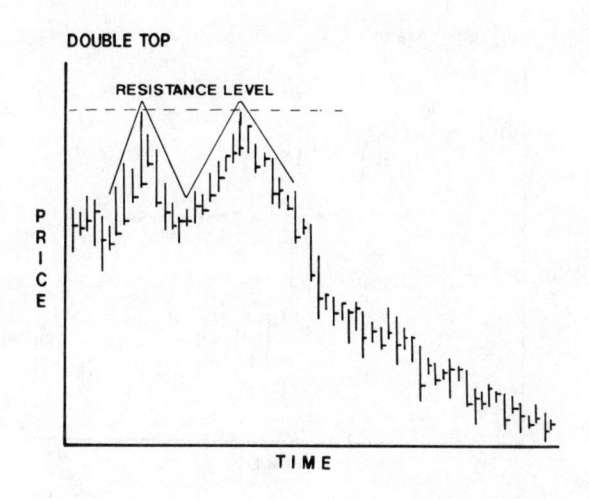

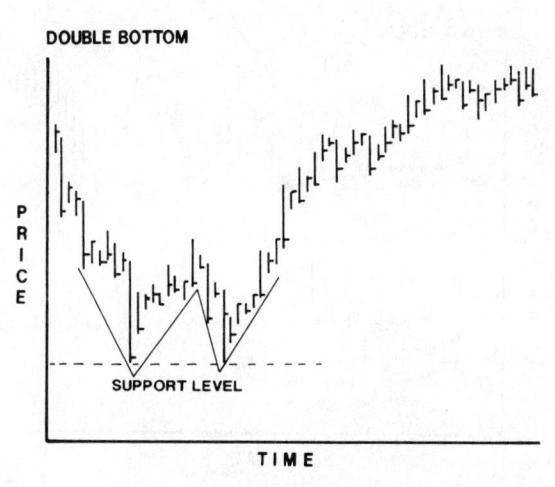

Figure 2-8. Double Signals

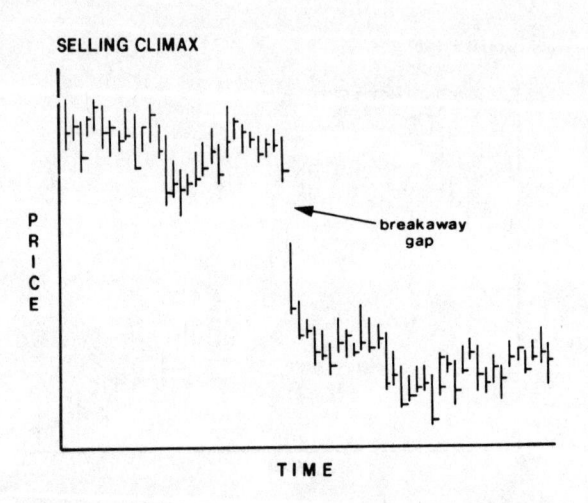

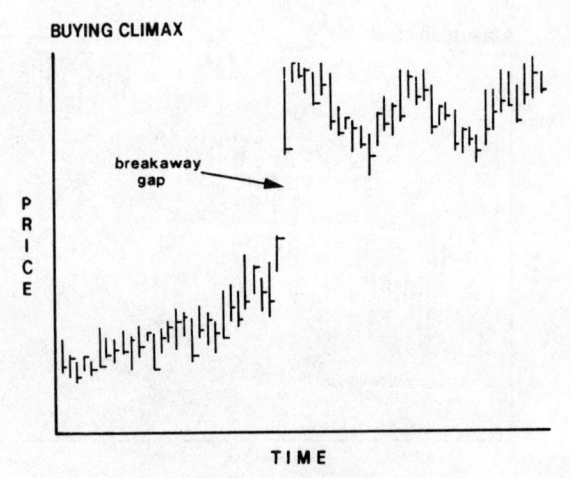

Figure 2-9. Climax Pattern

certainly improve your perceptions of how the market works. However, it would be a mistake to attach too much importance to either complicated mathematical models or simplistic theories, or to assume that a past trend will always dictate the future.

The reality is that the market reacts or overreacts to news and price movement in an unpredictable manner. You can believe the claims, made by some, that are based on a look backward, but don't invest just on the basis of such proof. You will find that looking forward is always more difficult. To be a smart investor, use fundamental and technical analysis to help you make a decision, but never use them as the last word.

3

INVESTIGATING COMPANIES

Take nothing on its looks; take everything on evidence. There's no better rule.

Charles Dickens

As an investor, you face many questions. When do you buy and sell? How much and where should you diversify? Whose advice should you take?

The first question most of us must face, however, is how to find out about companies. We will be investing in common stock traded on the public exchanges, which represents proportionate ownership in corporations. Common stock is the best-known investment; yet, many individuals buy it on the basis of unsubstantiated recommendations, hunches, or criteria entirely unrelated to a defined standard for risk.

If you start out like most investors, you will probably take the advice of your stockbroker. But that can be a mistake if, like most people new to investing, you have a stockbroker who is also new to the game.

This chapter discusses various types of research for selection of common stock investments. It also tells you where to find free or low-cost information about companies.

In addition to investigating companies, you must also be willing to explore the investment product itself. Start with the fundamentals, not as the sole means for choosing one stock over another, but to:

1. Establish a valid comparison between two or more candidate stocks.
2. Eliminate stocks that clearly do not meet your risk standards.
3. Expand selection criteria beyond an outside recommendation or a preliminary measure of a stock's potential growth.

BROKER RESEARCH

Make a distinction between your broker's research and his recommendations. Typically, a broker calls you and makes a sales pitch: "I'm looking at the stock of a very promising company. I think you should buy 100 shares."

Many investors assume that such a recommendation is the result of extensive and careful research, but that is not always the case. Often, brokers are told to recommend a stock because the brokerage firm, acting as an underwriter, has bought a large block of shares at a discounted price and must now sell those shares at retail. By the time you hear about the stock, the real bargain has probably already passed. Other investors have bought shares at a low price (relative to the current market price), and the opportunity, for you, has been lost.

Follow this rule:

> Never buy just because a broker makes a recommendation to you. First, look at the information your broker should offer to back up that recommendation.

The larger brokerage firms put a lot of time and effort into research. They have entire departments dedicated to investigating new and existing companies; judging their current performance, management, earnings record, and other important factors; and estimating their future prospects.

The research a brokerage firm conducts may be quite comprehensive, going far beyond historical trends and projections of future earnings, dividends, and market price. The research is based on:

- Interviews with specialists who buy and sell the stock and know the inside workings of the company and the industry.
- Discussions with top managers in the company, the decision makers who establish the direction the company will take in the future.
- Investigation of stock owned by insiders, such as top executives in the company, and their recent volume of buy or sell orders.
- The competition, and the company's ability to attract and keep its market share.

This is more information than most of us have when we decide to invest; so being able to get copies of research reports is helpful to anyone considering buying stock in a company.

The research report should provide you with the researcher's in-depth evaluation of the company and its prospects for growth. A thorough report will discuss the various fundamental factors, including financial status, growth potential, and strength of the organization next to its competitors. It will also explain how well management is doing, not only in managing the company and marketing its product or service, but also in its relationships with employees, vendors, creditors, labor unions, and stockholders.

Look for companies with highly favorable research reports. Avoid investing in the stock of a company whose management has turned over several times during the past few years or whose profit and sales growth trend has been very inconsistent. Also avoid investing in companies that are undergoing problems with labor unions or that have large lawsuits pending.

There is a difference between an in-depth, objective research report and a brokerage firm's marketing report. The latter is probably a one-page summary of the company with a buy or hold recommendation printed on the top. It only summarizes the business the company is in and gives the researcher's reasons why it's a good investment. You should look beyond the marketing report.

Example: You request research reports on two companies in the same industry. Your broker mails them to you and you begin your review and comparison. One company is identified as the leader in its industry. Sales have been growing at a steady pace for many years; the gross margin and net profit margins have remained nearly the same for the year; and the dividend rate and earnings per share have not changed substantially. Management has undergone few changes in the last five years, and the outlook is for a strong future.

The second company has experienced less stable growth. Over a five-year period, three years showed a nice profit, but two reported net losses. The dividend was excluded for the last two years, and earnings per share have been inconsistent. The report explains that top management has been changed several times and that a principal labor union is threatening a strike in the near future.

By comparing both companies, you can determine which one is a likely candidate for you. Even though the second company's stock appears to have grown at a better rate, its other fundamentals show much less stability and leadership.

If you work with a brokerage firm, ask for copies of its research reports on companies it recommends to you. If none are available, ask these questions to classify stocks in terms of risk:

1. On what basis are you suggesting I buy the stock?
2. What is the five-year record of the major fundamental indicators (earnings per share, average P/E ratio, net profit, sales, and strength in the industry, for example)?
3. How does this company compare to its major competitors in terms of consistent growth and margin of profit?
4. What do you estimate will be this stock's average trading range two, three, and four years from now?

In choosing a brokerage firm in which to open an account, first ask to see the type of research the company has available. A brokerage firm with an extensive research department will be able to supply you with a current report on the most actively traded stocks or on those issues it considers good prospects in the near future.

As with all investment decisions, never invest under pressure. Insist on in-depth reports before buying stock and do not depend just on the broker's advice. Do not pass up the important investigative phase because you have been told that timing is essential.

Investing under pressure is a highly speculative approach. Speculation is making an investment strictly to earn a high amount of profit in the shortest possible time. To achieve this end, a speculator must be willing to assume much greater risks than the long-term investor. In fact, the speculator seeks out the highest-risk investments (in terms of price volatility, for example) because they also have the greatest potential for gain.

Speculation is one of many strategies. As a general rule, only the most experienced investors can afford to speculate, and then will do so only with a portion of their total funds. Most speculators put only a small portion of their capital at maximum risk, leaving the balance in more secure investments.

By diversifying and isolating a small portion of your total portfolio for speculation, a loss—even a big one—will not be completely devastating. Speculation is a poor approach only if the investor does not understand the risks involved or cannot afford the potential losses. The appeal of fast riches and the excitement of high risk attract many people to excessive speculation. An intelligent way to accept high risk is to devote part of your cash to the speculation game and put the remainder in longer-term, more conservative investments.

INDEPENDENT RESEARCH

To many investors, a brokerage firm's research is not as objective as it should be. If the firm stands to gain when its customers buy, how fairly can it report? And, of course, the typical commission-based firm must depend on buying and selling volume to earn a profit.

One alternative is to subscribe to an independent research service. A firm that specializes in providing investors with in-

52   *Investor Factline*

formation might be more objective because it earns money from good advice, not from commissions.

Besides pointing out bargains or companies with a strong competitive edge, an independent research company can also point out weaknesses. Its real value to you as a subscriber will be in forecasting not only buying opportunities but risks and slow markets, and in showing how current economic and market trends can affect you in the future.

The most in-depth independent research is provided by the "Value Line Investment Survey," a market subscription service that tracks 1700 stocks and watches industry trends. It uses a ranking system that compares the timeliness and safety of each publicly traded company.

Value Line gives its subscribers a great deal of research. It offers a trial subscription of 10 weeks, so that you will not have to pay a lot of money to judge the value of the service. You receive a one-page summary for each of the 1700 stocks, as well as weekly updates, a summary and index, and a commentary on each week's trends.

The ranking system works in this way: Both safety and timeliness are ranked from 1 to 5, with 1 indicating the best chance for stability and performance. Over many years, the higher-ranked stocks have, as a group, out-performed the lower-ranked stocks.

Figure 3-1 shows a sample page from "Value Line Investment Survey" from 1988.[1]

The top line gives the name of company, the exchange where it trades, the most recent price, the P/E ratio, and the dividend yield. Immediately below and on the left is a brief history of the corporation and its capital structure. In the top middle portion of the page is a price chart over a 10-year period, with inset boxes for insider buy and sell decisions, and another box for institutional activity (purchases, sales, and holdings of mutual funds and other institutions). At the far right is the target price range for two to five years out.

On the top right-hand side is the important Value Line

---

1. Copyright © 1988 by Value Line, Inc.; used by permission.

CLUB MED, INC. NYSE-CMI

RECENT PRICE	P/E RATIO	RELATIVE P/E RATIO	DIV'D YLD	VALUE LINE
14	10.0 (Trailing: 11.6 / Median: NMF)	0.78	1.4 %	1755

Club Med, Inc. was incorporated on May 17, 1984 in the Cayman Islands, British West Indies as a wholly-owned subsidiary of Club Mediterranee S.A., a French public company. The company is successor to the operations of the parent in the United States, Mexico, the Caribbean, Asia, the South Pacific and the Indian Ocean; Club Mediterranee continues to operate Club Med resorts elsewhere in the world. The parent company's ownership was reduced to 73% by a public sale of stock in September 1984. In that initial public offering, the sale of 3.4 million shares at $17.00 was underwritten by Shearson Lehman/American Express, E.F. Hutton, et al.

The shares were directly listed on the New York Stock Exchange.

Club Med markets packages that provide complete prepaid vacations at its various self-contained resort villages, typically located in beach or mountain settings. Each village offers activites primarily sports oriented; evening entertainment is cabaret/night club/Broadway style; for late night hours, there are discotheques.

	1984	1985	1986	1987
High	17.8	26.4	32.3	29.3
Low	14.8	16.0	21.3	9.0

Insider Decisions 1987

	N	D	J	F	M	A	M	J	J	A	S	O	N	D	J
to Buy	0	0	0	0	0	0	0	0	0	0	0	0	0	0	0
Options	0	0	0	0	0	0	0	0	0	0	0	0	0	0	0
to Sell	0	0	0	0	0	0	0	0	0	0	0	0	0	0	0

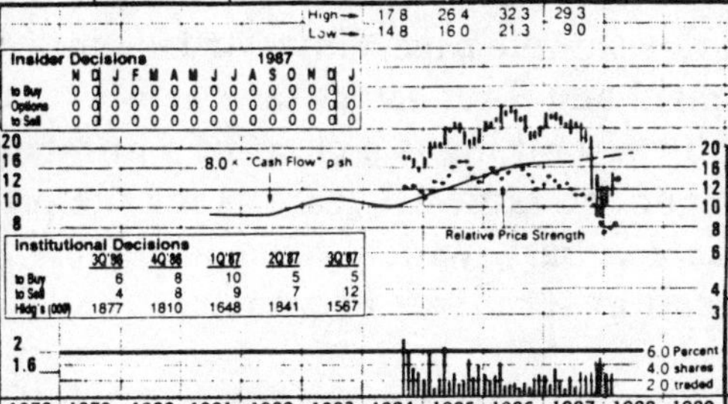

Institutional Decisions

	3Q'86	4Q'86	1Q'87	2Q'87	3Q'87
to Buy	6	8	10	5	5
to Sell	4	8	9	7	12
Hldg's (000)	1877	1810	1648	1841	1567

March 11, 1988 — Value Line

TIMELINESS (Relative Price Performance Next 12 Mos.) **4** Below Average

SAFETY (Scale: 1 Highest to 5 Lowest) **3** Average

BETA .95 (1.00 = Market)

1990-92 PROJECTIONS

	Price	Gain	Ann'l Total Return
High	35	(+ 150%)	27%
Low	20	(+ 45%)	11%

1978	1979	1980	1981	1982	1983	1984	1985	1986	1987	1988	1989	© VALUE LINE, INC.	90-92E
--	--	--	18.03	20.67	21.15	17.17	20.41	24.50	26.18	**28.30**		Sales per sh (A)	39.65
--	--	--	1.16	1.15	1.42	1.28	1.61	2.10	2.14	**2.40**		"Cash Flow" per sh	3.35
--	--	--	.77	.69	.94	1.09	1.04	1.27	1.19	**1.40**		Earnings per sh (B)	2.00
--	--	--	--	--	--	--	.20	.20	.20	**.21**		Div'ds Decl'd per sh (C)	.40
--	--	--	.99	.44	1.16	2.19	4.57	3.00	3.26	**2.00**		Cap'l Spending per sh	4.15
--	--	--	4.17	4.15	5.62	9.45	10.40	11.56	13.02	**14.50**		Book Value per sh	19.30
--	--	--	10.00	10.00	10.00	13.70	13.71	13.75	14.15	**14.15**		Common Shs Outst'g (D)	14.50
--	--	--	--	--	--	16.0	19.9	20.3	20.6	Bold figures are Value Line estimates		Avg Ann'l P/E Ratio	14.0
--	--	--	--	--	--	1.49	1.62	1.38	1.36			Relative P/E Ratio	1.15
--	--	--	--	--	--	--	1.0%	.8%	.8%			Avg Ann'l Div'd Yield	1.5%
--	--	--	180.3	206.7	211.5	235.3	279.7	337.0	370.4	**400**		Sales ($mill) (A)	575
--	--	--	6.3%	6.4%	7.8%	9.0%	8.5%	9.3%	9.1%	**9.0%**		Operating Margin	9.0%
--	--	--	3.6	4.3	4.5	6.1	7.8	11.5	13.5	**14.0**		Depreciation ($mill)	20.0
--	--	--	7.9	7.1	9.7	11.5	14.2	17.4	16.8	**19.8**		Net Profit ($mill)	29.0
--	--	--	11.2%	21.0%	11.5%	14.2%	15.6%	9.0%	3.7%	**5.0%**		Income Tax Rate	9.0%
--	--	--	4.4%	3.5%	4.6%	4.9%	5.1%	5.2%	4.5%	**5.0%**		Net Profit Margin	5.0%
--	--	--	--	d.4	6.2	34.6	31.9	30.9	4.6	**20.0**		Working Cap'l ($mill)	30.0
--	--	--	--	33.7	59.4	39.3	76.1	91.2	89.4	**95.0**		Long-Term Debt ($mill)	130
--	--	--	41.7	41.5	56.2	129.5	142.5	159.0	184.2	**205**		Net Worth ($mill)	280
--	--	--	19.0%	9.7%	8.9%	7.1%	7.5%	8.2%	7.1%	**9.5%**		% Earned Total Cap'l	8.0%
--	--	--	19.0%	17.2%	17.2%	8.9%	10.0%	10.9%	9.1%	**9.5%**		% Earned Net Worth	10.5%
--	--	--	19.0%	17.2%	17.2%	8.9%	8.1%	9.2%	7.6%	**8.5%**		% Retained to Comm Eq	8.5%
--	--	--	--	--	--	--	19%	16%	17%	**15%**		% All Div'ds to Net Prof	20%

CAPITAL STRUCTURE as of 10/31/87
Total Debt $105.9 mill. **Due in 5 Yrs** $79.0 mill.
LT Debt $89.4 mill. **LT Interest** $7.8 mill.
Incl. $6.0 mill. capitalized leases.
(Total interest coverage: 3.5x) (33% of Cap'l)
Guarantees affiliates' debt: $11.8 mill.

Leases, Uncapitalized Annual rentals $8.0 mill.
Pension Liability None in '87 vs. None in '86
Pfd Stock None

Common Stock 14,146,000 shs. (67% of Cap'l)

CURRENT POSITION ($MILL.)	1985	1986	10/31/87
Cash Assets	47.5	53.6	29.7
Receivables	14.4	15.4	23.5
Inventory(Avg Cst)	7.4	8.3	11.9
Other	9.1	13.8	15.8
Current Assets	78.4	91.1	80.9
Accts Payable	10.0	12.1	8.8
Debt Due	3.8	2.4	16.5
Other	32.7	45.7	51.0
Current Liab.	46.5	60.2	76.3

ANNUAL RATES of change (per sh)	Past 10 YEARS	Past 5 YEARS	Est'd '85-'87 to '90-'92
Sales	—	4.5%	11.0%
"Cash Flow"	—	12.0%	11.5%
Earnings	—	10.0%	11.5%
Dividends	—	8.0%	17.5%
Book Value	—	26.0%	10.5%

Fiscal Year Ends	QUARTERLY SALES ($ mill.) (A) Jan. 31	Apr. 30	July 31	Oct. 31	Full Fiscal Year
1984	62.1	76.0	47.6	49.6	235.3
1985	71.9	87.3	62.3	58.2	279.7
1986	85.4	107.9	73.5	70.2	337.0
1987	97.1	114.1	78.1	81.1	370.4
1988	**105**	**125**	**85.0**	**85.0**	**400**

Fiscal Year Ends	EARNINGS PER SHARE (A) Jan. 31	Apr. 30	July 31	Oct. 31 (B)	Full Fiscal Year
1984	.26	.95	d.17	.05	1.09
1985	.34	.97	d.18	d.09	1.04
1986	.38	1.08	d.17	d.02	1.27
1987	.41	1.11	d.29	d.04	1.19
1988	**.43**	**1.20**	**d.19**	**d.04**	**1.40**

Calendar	DIVIDENDS PAID (C) Mar. 31	June 30	Sept. 30	Dec. 31	Full Year
1984	--	--	--	--	--
1985	.10	--	.10	--	.20
1986	.10	--	.10	--	.20
1987	.10	--	.10	--	.20
1988	.10				

BUSINESS: Club Med, Inc. operates 25 resorts in the United States, Mexico, Caribbean, Asia, South Pacific and Indian Ocean areas. Sells vacation packages (69% of revenues) and air transportation (27%) to "villages" offering sports and entertainment activities. 10/87 bed capacity: North America 1,030 (56.5% average occupancy); Mexico-Caribbean 9,068 (60.4%); Asia 3,250 (58.2%). Average plant age: 4 years. 1987 depreciation rate: 4.7%. Payroll estimated 50% of sales. Employs about 5,000; has 860 shareholders. Club Mediterranee S.A. (France) owns 73%. Chairman: Gilbert Trigano. President: Jacques Giraud. Incorporated: Cayman Islands, BWI. Address: 40 West 57th Street, New York, NY 10019. Telephone: 212-977-2100.

Club Med patrons must have been out of the October market. Bookings by vacationers for the current winter season have remained strong despite the late 1987 plunge in stock prices. Partial recovery in the trading levels for Club Med shares from their year-end lows tends to confirm that investors overreacted to concerns about how the company would be affected. Present indications are that no recession fears will prevent revenue and profit growth for Club Med in the fiscal year ending October 31, 1988. Absent tangible evidence of a turnabout from the recent earnings downtrend, however, the stock is not ranked favorably for year-ahead market performance.

Year-end 1987 gains were offset by special charges. Fourth-quarter adjustments for this company stand out prominently because something less than break-even is the best that can be expected for the off-season second half. Club Med's final 1987 fiscal quarter included a gain of 12¢ a share on the sale of the Fort Royal village in Guadeloupe, and 5¢ on switching to a new type of pension plan. Value Line would exclude these nonrecurring items from the data presentation if there had not been a substantially equivalent adverse impact from the stronger French franc on personnel and overhead charges allocated by parent Club Mediterranee.

A four-year expansion push is nearing completion. The capital investment program launched in 1984 to add, enlarge and modernize resort villages now totals $180 million. The $46.2 million expended last year helped to complete Bali in Indonesia, Huatalco in Mexico, and Sandpiper in Florida. Some of it also went into expansion and renovations at Playa Blanca in Mexico; Paradise Island in the Bahamas; and the Caravelle Village on Guadeloupe, which was acquired from the parent company for 382,950 shares.

A flatter cost uptrend will ease margin pressures. Last year's 59.6% occupancy rate indicates sizable room for enlarging revenues even though the facilities expansion pace winds down. The 8% increment in beds, which brought the total to 13,350, was not available for generating income all through 1987, while the interest expense, staff training and related expansion costs were being absorbed. *Edmund B. Swort*

(A) Fiscal year ends October 31st of calendar year. (B) Based on average shares outstanding. Excludes extraordinary and nonrecurring credits: '84, 5¢; '85, 10¢; '86, 5¢; '87, 4¢. Next earnings report due late March. (C) Next dividend meeting about Aug. 9. Goes ex about Aug. 29. Dividend payment dates: about Feb. 17, Sept. 15. (D) In millions.

Company's Financial Strength	B+
Stock's Price Stability	55
Price Growth Persistence	NMF
Earnings Predictability	35

Factual material is obtained from sources believed to be reliable, but the publisher is not responsible for any errors or omissions contained herein.

Figure 3-1. A Sample Page from "Value Line Investment Survey" from 1988 ranking. In this sample page, Club Med is ranked 4 for timeliness (below average) and 3 for safety (average).

Beneath the ranking is a chart of a number of fundamental indicators over the same 10 years as for the price chart. This is a very valuable chart, which you can review at a glance with specific selection standards in mind.

Example: You have determined that a likely candidate must have consistent growth in net sales per share, earnings per share, and dividend payments. Applying these rules to Club Med, you would conclude the following:

- Net sales per share have risen steadily over the history of the company.
- Earnings per share have also risen since 1981.
- Dividends have been paid at the rate of 20 cents per share for the last three years.

Below the statistical fundamentals are actual sales, operating margin, profit, and other financial summaries. Some points to review in this section:

- Sales, operating margin (profit after costs but before expenses), and net profits have all continued to grow—a sign of consistent management.
- Net profit margin has been consistent within a very minor range of variance, averaging about 5 percent per year.

To the far left and below the fundamental summaries is a summary of assets, liabilities, and net worth (the balance sheet information), and quarterly summaries of sales, earnings per share, and dividends.

Below the fundamentals and from the center to the right side of the page are the narrative sections. The first section describes the company's major business, including the number of outlets, employees, sources of revenues, and so forth. The second section is an analysis of the company's prospects. Here are mentioned any special circumstances, such as labor union problems, large pending lawsuits, or pressure from competitors. Any positive aspects of the business are also listed. In this case, the researcher notes that although bookings remained strong during the slow season, investors seem to have overreacted to the October 1987 crash. In the researcher's opinion, the stock will not perform well in the coming year. This section also mentions that 1987 gains were offset by nonrecurring adjustments and the effects of foreign exchange rates.

The same kind of comprehensive summary is given for each of the 1700 stocks in the "Value Line Investment Survey," among which are most of the largest corporations with which investors are familiar. The service also gives subscribers a weekly summary listing the most conservative stocks, the highest-yielding stocks, the stocks with the highest 3- to 5-year appreciation, the best performing stocks during the latest 13-week period, the lowest and highest price/earnings ratios, and the highest dividend yields. The summary includes a ranking of industry groups.

Because Value Line analyzes its 1700 stocks in so many ways, subscribers can make comparisons and evaluations based on any combination of fundamental and technical indicators they want. The service does not recommend any one method for selecting stocks; it provides updated information of the most valuable kind and leaves it to the investor to interpret it.

Value Line is extensive and affordable, but it is limited to only the 1700 stocks on its list. Nevertheless, this is preferable to a service that covers a broader market with less information.

Another research subscription service worth considering is "The Outlook," offered by Standard & Poor's Corporation. This service offers a 12-page weekly report about the market that includes recent trends and provides information on companies it thinks investors should look at. Each report also contains a Forecast and Policy section breaking down current opportunities and risks in the market; features on investment selection techniques; lists of recommended issues; and statistical highlights.

Both "Value Line Investment Survey" and "The Outlook" are advertised regularly in the major financial newspapers and magazines, and both offer trial subscriptions. For information write to:

The Value Line Investment Survey
711 Third Avenue
New York, NY 10017

Standard & Poor's Corporation
25 Broadway
New York, NY 10004

AUTOMATED RESEARCH

Finding research quickly might have been a problem in the past, but today, anyone with a home computer and a modem can easily, and relatively cheaply, find what he needs through a networking program.

Now, you can get up-to-the-minute stock quotes, the latest news on a portfolio of stocks, research and analysis reports, and other information, all on your own home computer screen. You can even enter your own trades without having to call your broker. Of course, you will have to pay for these privileges. The subscription fee, telephone charges, and, most of all, a rate charged by the minute or by the hour for online access can add up quickly.

The two best-known online services for the investor are:

1. *Dow Jones News/Retrieval*
This service provides stock quotes, portfolio tracking, breaking news, analysis, financial overviews and statements, dividends and interest rates, online trading (in cooperation with your brokerage firm), corporate profiles, and earnings reports and forecasts. (Address: P.O. Box 300, Princeton, NJ 08540)

2. *CompuServe Information Services*
This is the largest networking database service, in terms of both information and the number of subscribers. It provides updated financial information, analysis and research, The Associated Press news service, and information filed by companies with the SEC. (Address: 500 Arlington Centre Blvd., Columbus, OH 43220)

Many brokerage firms use these online databases to support their own software. For example, Charles Schwab & Company, the largest discount broker in the United States, offers a service called SchwabQuotes that provides automatic quotes on stocks and access to the Dow Jones News/Retrieval system for updated news and analysis.

Dow Jones & Company markets two products besides its News/Retrieval: *Market Manager Plus*, a system for keeping records of your portfolio; and *Market Analyzer*, software that enables you to build price and volume charts. Both programs are updated automatically through the News/Retrieval system.

If you are interested in evaluating and comparing investment software, consider joining the American Association of Individual Investors (612 North Michigan Avenue, Chicago, IL 60611). This organization publishes a 216-page book, which it gives free to members, entitled *Microcomputer Resource Guide*. Also consider membership in the National Association of Investors Corporation (P.O. Box 220, Royal Oak, MI 48068). This association publishes *Better Investing* 10 times per year, which features articles about new hardware and software and product reviews.

The value of an ongoing subscription is that new products, services, and capabilities are constantly emerging in the computer field. What is not available or too expensive today will be available and inexpensive tomorrow.

RESEARCHING OTHER INVESTMENTS

Automated investing is aimed primarily at the stock market, for two reasons. First, through direct purchase and the mutual fund industry, this is the most widely known and popular market. Second, it is public, so important information is readily available. This is not the case for every type of investment.

If you want to put your money in something other than stocks, you'll need to find your research elsewhere. For example, a service called "Mutual Fund Values" provides subscribers with weekly information about 777 different funds.

Choosing any investment is a matter of comparison. That's where a service like "Mutual Fund Values" is useful. Not only does it provide in-depth statistical information; it also compares the management fees, sales charges, and other information about fund purchases that is hard to find in the typical prospectus.

Many large brokerage firms offer free booklets about investment products other than stocks, such as bonds, options, real estate partnerships, and other investments the firm sells. Also check current issues of investment magazines for specific information about areas of interest.

For free mutual fund information, write to the Investment Company Institute (1775 K Street, Washington DC 20006) for copies of its membership list (containing names, addresses, and investment objectives for most funds) and for the booklet "The Age-Old Question," a listing of the questions you should ask when shopping for a mutual fund.

Also write to the Consumer Information Center, P.O. Box 100, Pueblo, CO 81002, for the latest *Consumer Information Catalog*. Look for these free or low-cost publications:

- "Before You Say Yes: Fifteen Questions to Ask About Investments" (*free*)
- "Understanding Opportunities and Risks in Futures Trading" (*50 cents*)
- "What Every Investor Should Know" (*$1.25*)
- "Consumer's Resource Handbook" (*free*)

Another excellent source for free information is the Federal Reserve System. Write to the Public Affairs Department, Federal Reserve Bank of Dallas, Station K, Dallas, TX 75222, for the booklet, "United States Treasury Securities."

Also write to the Commodity Futures Trading Commission, 2033 K Street, N.W., Washington DC 20581, for free copies of:

- "Basic Facts About Commodity Futures Trading"
- "Glossary of Trading Terms"

Also check your local bank. Now that banks and savings and loan associations are becoming active in the investment industry, many offer free information about specific investment products.

NONSECURITY INVESTMENTS

The need for complete knowledge is critical for nonsecurity investments. Be especially wary about promotions for these products, which include collectibles (like stamps and coins), precious metals, and gemstones. These are the areas where con artists are most likely to operate because their activities do not come under the jurisdiction of the SEC.

With all forms of nonsecurity investment, you face four problems you don't experience with stocks, bonds, and mutual funds.

1. No public marketplace

First, there is no orderly auction marketplace. Coins and stamps, for example, are traded through dealers and other collectors, who set prices according to what they think the market will bear. Stock prices, on the other hand, are set purely by daily supply and demand, and the industry is highly regulated.

2. The need for expertise

Second is the problem of expertise. To trade in the exotic forms of investment, you must be an expert or you will eventually have a big loss. Expertise does not mean just being able to time trades to produce profits. It also means being thoroughly aware of what creates value. A stamp or coin collector must be able to recognize a forgery, tell similar stamps apart, and estimate grades of value. This requires experience and study.

Example: The 1984 value of an 1892-S Morgan silver dollar was $20,000 if graded Mint State-65, or $4,500 if graded MS-60. The grading is so close, however, that only an experienced and trained eye might be able to tell the difference.

Knowledge is essential in this market; without it you cannot succeed. In the stock market, that is not always true. You are most likely to succeed in any investment if you know what you're doing, but it's still possible to earn profits when you know relatively little about stocks and their analysis.

3. The self-interest of dealers

To listen to most dealers, "now" is always the best time to buy, whether now is today, tomorrow, or a year down the road. You will never hear a dealer say, "This is not a good time to buy."

If the prices of a collectible are rising rapidly, dealers urgently suggest buying. And if prices have fallen, they compare today's bargains to the high prices of the past.

4. The cost of investing

The fourth problem is that of markup and markdown when you buy and sell through a dealer. Even with an impressive increase in market value, it is difficult to make a profit because of the high cost going in and out of the investment.

For example, if you buy an investment-grade coin through a dealer, you will have to pay a markup commission of approximately 20 percent. Later, when you sell, you will be charged a markdown commission of about 30 percent. Assuming you purchase your coin for $400 and it increases in value by 70 percent in one year, how much net profit will you make?

Purchase price	$400
Plus: 20% markup	80
Total price	$480
Sale price (70% increase)	$680
Less: 30% markdown	$204
Net sale price	$476
Net loss	$ −4

Instead of earning a 70 percent return, you lose $4 on a $480 investment. Still, the ads for that coin will continue to claim that "values increased 70 percent last year."

Buying specialized investments, including coins, stamps, antiques, rare art, or collectible books, requires expertise beyond investment knowledge. You must also be an expert in the particular field and know how to spot values.

Investment-grade collectibles can be found at trade shows, where investors and collectors trade among themselves. Here some real bargains can be found—as long as you truly know what to look for.

If you have the expertise to become involved in nonsecurity investments, you can earn a very decent profit over time. Because supplies are limited, the potential for gains over time is significant. The other aspect of investing in collectibles is personal satisfaction: A rare gold coin is much more pleasing to look at than a stock certificate, and a mounted rare stamp gives more pleasure than a monthly statement from a mutual fund.

PROTECTING YOUR OWN INTERESTS

Any investment must be thoroughly understood before the right decision can be made. For collectibles, you must have a special level of expertise. For publicly traded stocks or mutual funds, you must know which questions to ask and how to apply information against your own investing standards. If a broker makes a recommendation, you should see the report on which it is based. If no report exists, turn to one of the independent research organizations; write to the company itself and ask for its annual report (see the next chapter); and perform your own thorough research.

Follow these guidelines whenever you invest:

1. Never make a decision in response to an unsolicited approach, especially if it comes to you by mail or by phone. Legitimate investments are never sold in this manner.
2. Find out the true cost of investing. Be sure you know the commission rate and other fees you will have to pay before buying or selling.
3. Always read the prospectus, not just the sales literature.
4. If in doubt, show material you receive to your stockbroker, accountant, or attorney. Ask for a second opinion.

5. Never invest under pressure. A true long-term opportunity will be there tomorrow and next month. If you want to put together a sound program, you must have all of the facts before you send in your money.
6. Ask all the right questions. A legitimate solicitation is one in which all information is made available to you without hesitation.
7. Guide your decisions by knowledge, not impulse. Resist the natural tendency to chase fast profits and concentrate on your own goals and risk standards.

In the next chapter, you will see how the annual report can be used to help you identify opportunities and dangers, and how to find more in-depth financial information than what is contained in the publicly distributed statements.

4

THE ANNUAL REPORT

Beware of all enterprises that require new clothes.

Henry David Thoreau

Annual reports are produced by all publicly held corporations as a way to summarize the year's results for stockholders. Similar reports are sent by syndication managers, Real Estate Investment Trusts (REITs), and other forms of investment.

These reports are primarily financial summaries of the year, but there's a lot more to them. They also include a message from the president or chairman of the board, extensive footnotes to the financial statements, the auditor's statement, and summaries of business activities and projects underway in each division.

You are not likely to find an annual report that contains bad news. Even when business has been poor, when there has been a loss instead of a profit, and when debt keeps rising while sales fall, the tone of the message is invariably positive.

You must develop the ability to read between the lines if the annual statement is to be of any use to you. For example, one company's sales were off drastically. Debt was rising, and the company was reporting a large loss for the third year in a row. Because it had cut its overhead, the loss was lower than in previous years, but the news was still very bad. Nevertheless, in the message from the president was the following comment:

> The move toward profitability has been underscored by the reduction of losses by over 50 percent as compared to the prior year.

THE AUDITOR'S LETTER

To really understand what the annual report tells you, first ignore the artistic impression it makes. A nicely prepared report, with balanced pages, multicolored graphs, and attractive photographs means only one thing: the company spent a lot of money and put in a great deal of effort. Chances are, though, that the majority of the report was written by a public relations firm rather than by people inside the company.

Get down to what the annual report actually says, how it reports the negatives, and what that means to you as an investor. Start by reading the auditor's letter, which follows the financial statements and is probably located in the back of the report. The standard letter states three points:

1. The books were audited using generally accepted accounting and auditing standards.
2. The report summarizes the financial condition and results of operations fairly and accurately.
3. There have been no changes in the methods of reporting that affect the accuracy of the report.

These are the statements made in the standard letter, when there are no problems. The letter assures you that the report is accurate. However, if any qualifications beyond these standard statements appear in the auditor's letter, that could spell trouble. A qualified opinion—indicated by a carefully worded letter that goes beyond the standard assurances—could be a sign that the company is headed for problems.

The letter is not going to state outright that the company is going out of business, that accounting practices are inaccurate, or that debt is too high. But it sends a warning just in the fact that it is more than the standard letter. Before you invest, you should find out more. That means checking the reports the company has sent to the SEC (more on this later in this chapter).

An example of a standard letter:

> We have examined the consolidated balance sheet of (company) as of (date), and the related consolidated statements of income,

changes in stockholders' equity, and changes in financial position for the 12 months ended (date). Our examination was made in accordance with generally accepted auditing standards and, accordingly, included such tests of the accounting records and other such auditing procedures as we considered necessary in the circumstances.

In our opinion, the aforementioned financial statements present fairly the financial position of (company) as of (date), and the results of operations and the changes in financial position for the twelve months then ended, in conformity with generally accepted accounting principles.

In a qualified opinion statement, the phrase "subject to" will probably appear. For example, the second paragraph of the statement above might read:

In our opinion, the aforementioned financial statements present fairly the financial position of (company) as of (date), and the results of operations and the changes in financial position for the twelve months then ended, in conformity with generally accepted accounting principles, subject to resolution of questions regarding capitalized valuation of patent rights claimed by the corporation, for which ownership is presently challenged and in litigation.

The part following the phrase "subject to" might be of such significance that the entire evaluation of the company is called into doubt. If, by directly contacting the company or studying research reports, you conclude that a problem has been resolved, then the qualification is satisfied. But if it's still pending, the danger signal is a clear one.

Qualification most frequently arises because the auditor does not agree with an interpretation made by management about valuation of an asset; methods of accounting; or the timing of income, costs, or expenses.

Example: A company values inventory on the basis of current market value, so that the asset value is greater than actual cost. The auditor argues that the inventory should be valued on the basis of cost, and neither side can agree.

Example: The company recognizes current income that, in the auditor's opinion, should be deferred until the year following.

Judging how significant a qualification is, in terms of whether you should invest, will depend on the nature of the problem. What is the effect on profits and profit trends? How much would a different interpretation of financial data affect future profitability and, ultimately, the stock's market price?

These questions should be addressed in research reports. A stockbroker recommending that you purchase shares should also have a specific answer to your questions. You can also refer your questions to your own accountant.

You may also write to the company directly and ask for more information about the qualification in the auditor's statement. Don't invest until you get satisfactory answers to all of your questions, and if that proves impossible, forget that stock and look at other companies whose audited statements show no disputes.

Keep in mind that even a standard auditor's statement is not a guarantee. The auditor only renders an opinion on whether the statements in the annual report are accurate. Even during the course of an extensive audit, the accountants do not check every transaction. They test-check a range of events, looking for big errors or misrepresentations, but they cannot always spot every incidence of error or fraud. Remember, too, that it is the company's management, and not the auditing firm, that decides which accounting principles to use during the year (accounting and inventory valuation methods, for example). The auditor only comments on whether those methods are fair and consistent.

When an auditing firm is ready to submit its report, a meeting takes place between the senior auditors and representatives of the company's management. Any problems that have been discovered are discussed at that time. In some instances, it is not unusual for some points to be *negotiated*.

Example: An auditing firm questions the company's method of estimating bad debts for the current year and the estimate of obsolete inventory. Also, it proposes several adjustments to reported profits. Management's response might be: "We'll revise our estimates of obsolete inventory if you agree to accept our bad debt numbers. And we'll also give in on the other adjustments you propose."

Because there is a give-and-take between management and the auditor, a standard auditing letter is not always the result of a truly independent opinion but, rather, one in which methods are judged, modified, and revised. These practices are not necessarily manipulative. Accounting standards are complex and subject to varied interpretation. Auditors often compromise with management in order to achieve a mutually acceptable version of accuracy.

MANIPULATING PROFITS

Some practices, though, are definitely manipulative, going beyond the question of interpretation. The Securities and Exchange Commission, among its other duties, oversees the financial reporting of publicly held corporations. In the reports of some corporations, it has discovered what it calls "cooking the books"—overstated profits and other questionable practices.

The incidence of outright fraud is rare, but accounting rules are complex enough that favorable interpretations can go a long way toward manipulating what gets reported to stockholders. Some examples:

Banking Earnings

Companies sometimes defer part of their profits (i.e., put off reporting them until the following year), a practice also referred to as "sugar bowling." Deferral helps even out year-to-year swings in profits reported to shareholders. It also pads against downturns in future periods, since low results can be offset by the banked earnings. This is deceptive because investors and would-be investors, reviewing trends over several years, are led to believe that growth is fairly stable, which is the way it should be. But the truth may be that it actually swings up and down from one year to the next.

Selection of Accounting Methods

Management has great leeway in its selection of accounting methods, and the choice affects earnings, often significantly. A positive earnings trend is in the best interest of management, whose performance is invariably judged on the basis of profits.

Selling and Buying Assets

The managers of a publicly held company might decide to sell a valuable capital asset during the year to boost reported profits. That in itself is not negative, but if the sale is used only to help make a positive report, it isn't always the best move for stockholders. Chances are, management is covering up an otherwise poor earnings report.

Management can also time the purchase of assets. The level of debt, cash flow, and deductions for depreciation are all affected by the timing of purchases.

Timing of Costs and Expenses

Executives are responsible for timing many of their costs and expenses. For example, machinery and equipment may be due for an expensive maintenance check this year, but profits are down. By deferring that expense until the following year, profits are preserved and expenses are delayed.

Revising Cost Estimates

To a degree, reported costs and expenses are estimated as of the date of a financial statement. For example, a company with a large balance in its accounts receivable must estimate how much is uncollectible. The higher that estimate, the lower the profit will be. So when profits need boosting, the estimate of bad debts will likely be lower.

When a company's management manipulates earnings, the stockholders almost always lose. The practice is self-serving, intended to protect the executive rather than the interests of the stockholders. And, there is ego at work: Executives want to succeed; they do not want to report losses or lower-than-expected earnings. The pressure is to always exceed earnings of previous years, to report larger volumes of sales, and to grow—regardless of whether this so-called improvement is a healthy long-term trend. In any event, it is certainly negative to report earnings that are lower than those projected. In some cases, temporary consolidation, slowing down of growth, and elimination of some lines of business are healthier for the company and for the stock's value.

How can you be certain that reported profits have not been manipulated? If a clever, experienced executive has carefully hidden the full truth, you probably will not be able to determine manipulation from the annual report. A huge fraud should be discovered by a complete audit, and the SEC also examines—and sometimes changes—what a corporation reports. The combination of independent auditing and regulatory oversight is intended to protect you from major fraud.

Even though you probably cannot detect a misrepresented financial report simply by reviewing it, you can judge historical earnings strength and consistency of operating results. When the gross sales, net profits, dividends, and net worth have all risen steadily over several years, that is a sign of a well-managed organization. But if profits and losses swing wildly from one year to the next, that is a more negative indicator.

An inconsistent result between years is not necessarily a sign that the books have been manipulated. Actual fraud is rare. But when two years showing moderate profits are followed by a third year reporting a large loss, chances are that the earlier results were interpreted in favor of the corporation.

Example: One company reported a $1.3 million profit two years ago, followed by a $12.9 million profit last year, and a $9.6 million loss this year. The footnotes to the financial statement explain that one-time adjustments were made during the current year. On average, the company earned about $1.5 million per year over the three-year period. If profits had been reported consistently during that period, you would now have a more dependable indicator of the trend and direction of the company.

An annual report is an important document that you should

always review. As a precaution, however, do not decide to invest in a company's stock *only* on the basis of what is shown there. Use it as one source of information. Do not limit your investigation to one or two years of financial information; look at the larger trend. Apply fundamental tests to judge financial strength (see the chapter on fundamental analysis), and compare the company's strength to the financial strength and profits of its competitors.

THE FOOTNOTE SECTION

After reviewing the auditor's opinion letter, check the footnotes to financial statements. While these might be complex and difficult to understand, they can also be very revealing. Footnotes expand on the numbers reported in the financial statements. Typically, they include explanations of:

1. Significant accounting policies

The footnotes explain how valuation of assets and reporting of transactions are done. Included are cash or accrual treatment of transactions, methods of depreciation, inventory valuation, methods for valuing investments the company holds, and the elimination of intercompany balances when reports are made on a consolidated basis.

2. Borrowings

Both short-term and long-term debt arrangements are described in footnotes. A faster rate of increase in debt than in the growth in profits for similar periods could be a sign of expansion, but it could also mean the company is experiencing cash flow difficulties. As debt grows so will interest payments, leading to a drain on cash flow in the future.

3. Unusual items

Unusual or extraordinary items are footnoted to qualify the reported profit or loss. For example, a company doing a lot of business overseas may have a profit or loss due to fluctuations in exchange rates. Or if a company must pay damages as part of a judgment against it, that will affect profits this year but will not be repeated in the future.

4. Stock options or warrants

This footnote explains employee incentive plans for the purchase of company stock. Options and warrants are a form of compensation and should be explained fully.

5. Contingent liabilities and commitments

Most large corporations are exposed to possible losses resulting from lawsuits, but these contingent liabilities are not reported on the financial statements until a judgment is actually entered against the company. Substantial pending suits should be listed and explained. Invariably, there is a statement to the effect that lawsuits "...in the opinion of management, will be resolved with no material effect on the consolidated statements or results of operations."

Commitments are similarly not reported on the financial statement. For example, a company has entered into a long-term lease agreement on its building or equipment. It will be required to pay $75,000 per year for the next 25 years. That is a substantial liability disclosed only in the footnotes and nowhere on the financial statements.

6. Valuation of assets

Capital assets are reported on the books on the basis of actual cost minus depreciation. But this formula is not always accurate. For example, a company buys an office building for $16 million and several years later, its depreciated value is $12 million. However, current market value might be $20 million or more. Footnotes explain the current market value versus reported book value of assets.

Besides the standard footnotes, look for unusual notes and statements. If the company has many pending lawsuits, declining sales with increasing debt, or significant changes in accounting methods, there is most likely a problem.

THE FINANCIAL STATEMENTS

The annual report always contains financial statements. The numbers reported for any one year are not as significant by themselves as they are in comparison to past years. So, besides current financial strength, you should look at the financial statements for trends: growth in sales and profits, earnings per share, and dividends; and stability in the rate of net profit.

These important points are discussed in more detail in Chapter 2, "Fundamental and Technical Analysis." For now, it is important only to understand what each statement reveals and what basic tests you can apply to them to judge one company against another.

There are several kinds of financial statements and related schedules in the annual report, including:

1. Balance sheet

This is a summary of assets, liabilities, and net worth as of the end of the fiscal year.

2. Income statement

This summarizes operations for the year, including sales, cost of goods sold, expenses, and profit or loss.

3. Statement of changes in financial position

Also called the "cash flow statement," this shows the sources and uses of funds during the year.

4. Changes in stockholders' equity

This shows the beginning balance, changes, and ending balance of net worth. Included are profits going to retained earnings, purchase and retirement of stock, dividends declared and paid, stock options exercised, and the issue of new classes of stock.

Some reports also break down income by subsidiary, costs and expenses, and other details not shown on the summarized statements. If the company has many subsidiaries, you should be able to identify profitability in each one as well as review the consolidated report.

Financial statements should always be given on a comparative basis in an annual report. Results for the current year and previous years should be listed. The more years shown, the better, since this enables you to spot trends and see what the rate of growth is.

Following is a simplified version of a company's balance sheet:

Sample Corporation
Consolidated Balance Sheet
December 31, 19__

	This year	Last year
Current assets:		
Cash	$ 627,850	$ 291,316
Accounts receivable	1,807,214	1,203,816
Inventory	935,190	985,190
Total	$3,370,254	$2,480,322
Long-term assets:	$2,903,410	$2,614,064
Less: depreciation reserve	(1,091,873)	(924,811)
Net	$1,811,537	$1,689,253
Intangible assets:		
Goodwill	$ 65,000	$ 65,000
Total assets	$5,246,791	$4,234,575
Current liabilities:		
Accounts payable	$1,162,335	$ 806,937
Taxes payable	68,419	94,400
Notes payable	448,932	448,932
Total	$1,679,686	$1,350,269
Long-term liabilities:		
Notes payable	$ 494,650	$ 945,016
Total liabilities	$2,174,336	$2,295,285
Stockholders' equity	$3,072,455	$1,939,290
Total liabilities and net worth	$5,246,791	$4,234,575

An explanation of each section:

Current Assets include all assets owned by the company that are in cash or are convertible to cash within one year.

Long-term Assets are the capital assets of the corporation, those that will be used beyond the year in which they are bought. They include buildings, equipment, machinery, furniture, autos, and trucks. The asset values are reduced each year by a corresponding expense for depreciation.

Intangible Assets are assets without physical value. "Goodwill" is an estimate of the value of the company's reputation. Other intangible assets include covenants not to compete and the estimated value of copyrights.

Current Liabilities include all debts payable within one year. The notes payable under this section represent 12 months of payments on all outstanding debts. When the company owes more than this amount, the balance is included in the next category.

Long-term Liabilities include all debts that are due beyond the coming 12 months.

Stockholders' Equity is the value of stock increased by the issue of new shares and net profits and reduced by losses and payment of dividends.

Balance sheets can include much more than these classifications. Prepaid assets (such as insurance premiums paid before they apply to the current period), deferred charges (expenses paid this year but applicable to the following year), and organizational expenses can be reported as assets. Liabilities can include "deferred credits," a classification for income received this year but not due to be earned until the next year.

A simplified version of a corporate income statement follows:

Sample Corporation
Consolidated Income Statement
For the year ended December 31, 19__

	This year	Last year
Gross sales	$18,470,035	$14,383,215
Cost of goods sold:		
Inventory, Jan. 1	$ 985,190	$ 1,005,930
Materials purchased	6,214,835	4,915,806
Direct labor	4,331,006	3,614,055
Other costs	218,483	230,814
Total	$11,749,514	$ 9,766,605
Less: inventory, Dec. 31	935,190	985,190
Cost of goods sold	$10,814,324	$ 8,781,415
Gross profit	$ 7,655,711	$ 5,601,800
Expenses:		
Selling expenses	$ 2,114,793	$ 1,632,815
General expenses	3,815,911	3,282,016
Total expenses	$ 5,930,704	$ 4,914,831
Net operating profit	$ 1,725,007	$ 686,969
Other income	$ 15,315	$ 32,515
Other expenses	(23,406)	(20,399)
Net profit before taxes	$ 1,716,916	$ 699,085
Federal income taxes	583,751	237,689
Net profit	$ 1,133,165	$ 461,396

An explanation of each section:

Gross Sales represent the total received or earned by the company. This line is often reduced by another category, "returns and allowances."

Cost of Goods Sold is that cost directly related to the generation of income. Note that the beginning and ending balances of inventory are included. The difference between them is an adjustment to direct costs; materials are purchased in excess of those used (increasing inventory levels), or part of inventory is used to generate income above and beyond current year purchases (thus reducing inventory levels).

Gross Profit is the amount remaining after deducting cost of goods sold from gross sales.

Expenses are divided between selling and general expenses (overhead). Selling expenses vary with the level of sales volume; general expenses are relatively fixed.

Net Operating Profit is the amount remaining after deducting total expenses from gross profit.

Other Income/Other Expenses include items such as interest, exchange rate fluctuations, capital gains or losses, and other sources of income and expense not part of company operations.

Net Profit Before Taxes is the balance of profit after adjusting for other income and expenses.

Federal Income Taxes represent an estimate of the amount the company owes to the government, based on the amount of profit and effective tax rates.

Net Profit is the bottom line, the amount of profit earned after all costs and expenses.

ANALYZING THE STATEMENT

Financial statement analysis is a complex field of study. An in-depth review, at any rate, will not always lead you to the best possible investment. The numbers are only one factor to consider in deciding whether to buy stock. A preliminary study of *trends* can point out strengths and weaknesses in a company, and a limited analysis is one effective way to compare one company with another.

Ratios should be applied to the balance sheet and income statement to compare, on three levels:

1. *The overall trend*

Ratios are meaningless by themselves; they must be developed and watched as part of a development over four or five years or more. Ratios are nothing more than summaries of the relationship between two numbers, which can help you to understand the trend itself.

2. *Strength*

How does one company compare with another? There is much more to the selection of a company's stock than just financial strength, but as one of many ways to pick a stock, comparative analysis of strength is a useful tool. For example, you are thinking of buying a stock in the data processing industry, and several companies are highly rated by research firms. Ratio tests will help you compare their financial strength.

3. *Standards*

Some ratios can be evaluated not only against past history and other companies but also against a well-understood norm. For example, if a certain type of company is expected to yield a 7 percent profit each year, you can judge an individual company's performance against that rate.

Six useful ratios are:

Current Ratio

This is the most common ratio of all. It is a comparison of current assets and current liabilities. The question asked by this ratio is "What level of current assets does the company hold for every dollar of current liability?"

The ratio is computed by dividing current assets by current liabilities. The answer is always expressed in the form "*x* to *1*." In the sample balance sheet, for example, we find that this year's current assets are $3,370,254 and current liabilities are $1,679,686. The current ratio is 2.01 to 1. (Figure 4-1)

As a general rule, a current ratio of 2 to 1 or better is con-

$$\frac{\text{current assets}}{\text{current liabilities}}$$

THIS YEAR	LAST YEAR
$\dfrac{\$3{,}370{,}254}{\$1{,}679{,}686} = 2.01 \text{ to } 1$	$\dfrac{\$2{,}480{,}322}{\$1{,}350{,}269} = 1.84 \text{ to } 1$

Figure 4-1. Current Ratio

sidered acceptable. Anything below that indicates the potential for cash flow problems. One point about current ratio, however: It is applicable only when companies carry significant levels of inventory. In our example, less than $1 million of inventory was reported, against sales of more than $18 million. That may not be a significant level.

Another point: In some very large corporations, the current ratio will be far below the 2 to 1 level. However, the sheer amount of available cash and consistent and steady profits in the organization make the ratio academic.

Quick Assets Ratio

This test is similar to the current ratio, except that it excludes inventories. It is an appropriate ratio when sales volume does not materially count on inventory levels or when the product is not kept in warehouses.

Also called the acid test or the liquidity ratio, the quick assets ratio is computed by dividing current assets (without inventory) by current liabilities. In the balance sheet example, this year's curent assets were $3,370,254 and inventory was $935,190. The difference, divided by current liabilities of $1,679,686, produces a quick assets ratio of 1.45 to 1. (Figure 4-2)

As a general standard, the quick assets ratio should be 1 to 1 or better. But, like the curent assets ratio, other factors can make the quick assets ratio a matter of little significance for very large companies. The trend in the ratio is more significant in most cases than the ratio by itself.

$$\frac{\text{current assets} - \text{inventory}}{\text{current liabilities}}$$

THIS YEAR

$$\frac{\$3{,}370{,}254 - \$935{,}190}{\$1{,}679{,}686} = 1.45 \text{ to } 1$$

LAST YEAR

$$\frac{\$2{,}480{,}322 - \$985{,}190}{\$1{,}350{,}269} = 1.11 \text{ to } 1$$

Figure 4-2. Quick Assets Ratio

Inventory Turnover

If inventory is a major factor in the control and growth of sales, the inventory turnover becomes an important ratio. It answers the question "How many times, on average, was inventory replaced during the year?"

This is an average only, indicating the degree of efficiency in inventory management. For example, if inventory includes many slow-moving and expensive items, the level will be too high and the turnover rate will slow down; and a too-small inventory will not be adequate to meet the demands of customers. The trend in inventory turnover is an important indicator, especially during periods of sales growth.

Inventory turnover is computed by dividing the cost of goods sold by average inventory for the period. The answer is always expressed in the number of average turns. For example, the cost of goods sold in the sample income statement was $10,814,324, and the average balance of inventory was $960,190 (based on the average between the beginning and ending inventory balances for the year). Cost of goods sold divided by average inventory equals 11.3 times. (Figure 4-3)

The average inventory can be computed on the basis of beginning and ending balances if levels are fairly stable during the year. However, if there are many changes in those levels due to seasonal factors, more frequent computations should be in-

$$\frac{\text{cost of goods sold}}{\text{average inventory}}$$

THIS YEAR

$$\frac{\$10{,}814{,}324}{\$960{,}190} = 11.3 \text{ times}$$

LAST YEAR

$$\frac{\$9{,}766{,}605}{\$995{,}560} = 9.81 \text{ times}$$

Figure 4-3. Inventory Turnover

cluded. For example, a quarterly inventory level, divided by four, can be used.

Some turnover computations are based on sales rather than cost of goods sold, but this is inaccurate. Sales are reported on a marked-up basis; inventory, on a cost basis.

Working Capital Turnover

Another important turnover computation is for working capital, which is defined as the difference between current assets and current liabilities.

The ratio answers the question "On average, how many times was working capital replaced during the year?" Admittedly, this is an inaccurate test, since current assets and liabilities are not actually replaced; they evolve. The ratio is a test of the averages, intended to spot directions and trends.

The value of this ratio is in showing how effective the company's internal controls are. During periods of growth, there is a tendency to allow accounts receivable and inventory levels to climb too high, which reduces the working capital ratio. It could be a sign that management is not controlling working capital.

The turnover is computed by dividing net sales by working capital. In the sample financial statements, this year's sales are $18,470,035, and working capital is $1,690,568. The working capital turnover ratio is 10.9 times. (Figure 4-4)

$$\frac{\text{gross sales}}{\text{working capital}}$$

THIS YEAR
$$\frac{\$18,470,215}{\$1,690,568} = 10.9 \text{ times}$$

LAST YEAR
$$\frac{\$14,383,215}{\$1,130,053} = 12.7 \text{ times}$$

Figure 4-4. Working Capital Turnover

Debt/Equity Ratio

This ratio compares total liabilities to tangible net worth. It shows the percentage of debts against shareholders' equity.

If debts begin climbing in comparison to equity, that is a negative sign. Corporations are capitalized from two sources: debt (money owed to others) and equity (the value of stock). There must be a consistent and controlled relationship between these two sources.

The ratio, expressed as a percentage, is computed by dividing liabilities by tangible net worth. "Tangible" means net worth reduced by any intangible assets. In the sample balance sheet, $65,000 was reported for goodwill, an amount that must be subtracted from the net worth (stockholders' equity) before computing the ratio. That leaves a balance of $3,007,455. Total liabilities of $2,174,336 divided by this total produce a debt/equity ratio of 72.3 percent. (Figure 4-5)

$$\frac{\text{liabilities}}{\text{tangible net worth}}$$

THIS YEAR
$$\frac{\$2,174,336}{\$3,007,455} = 72.3\%$$

LAST YEAR
$$\frac{\$2,295,285}{\$1,874,290} = 122.5\%$$

Figure 4-5. Debt/Equity Ratio

Return on Sales

This is, perhaps, the best understood of all ratios. Simply put, it is the percentage of sales that profits represent. Return on sales is computed by dividing net income by total sales. In the sample income statement, net income is $1,133,165, and total sales are $18,470,035. That produces a return on sales of 6.1 percent. (Figure 4-6)

The return-on-sales calculation should be compared over many years, but growth in the percentage is not a practical expectation. Most industries are limited by the percentage they can expect to earn; so an analysis of earnings per share of common stock is probably more valid. (This is discussed in detail in Chapter 2, "Fundamental and Technical Analysis.")

Return on sales is an important measure of a company's year, primarily because it is so well understood. Caution is advised, however, in comparing one company with another. Be sure that the comparison is for the same amount, and be aware that some companies report return on sales on the basis of net operating profit, on a pre-tax basis, or for periods of less than a full year. Also be aware that what is considered an acceptable rate of return varies from one industry to another.

$$\frac{\text{net income}}{\text{sales}}$$

THIS YEAR

$$\frac{\$1{,}133{,}165}{\$18{,}470{,}035} = 6.1\%$$

LAST YEAR

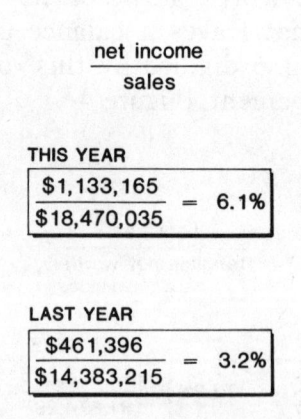

$$\frac{\$461{,}396}{\$14{,}383{,}215} = 3.2\%$$

Figure 4-6. Return on Sales

LOOKING BEYOND THE REPORT

Financial information in annual reports is a highly summarized version of what occurred during the year. The report shows what is required by law; it makes certain disclosures; and its statements are audited. But there's usually much more to a company than this.

Every publicly owned company is required to file annual and quarterly reports with the SEC, which contain many more details than does the annual report. If you are serious about buying stock, you should see these reports before you invest. Form 10-K is filed at the end of each year and form 10-Q at the end of every three months. These forms include historical information and points about operations that are often left out of the annual report entirely.

The 10-K must be filed within 90 days of the close of each year. It includes the names of principal stockholders and the number of shares they own. It discloses information about patents, licenses, and franchises that might never be mentioned in the annual report, and its disclosures tend to be more direct and have less of a public relations flavor to them. For example, in discussing expenditures for development of a new product, the 10-K report might state:

> Developmental expenses over the last four years have not resulted in a marketable product to date.

In the annual report, the same information might be rephrased to read:

> The company has dedicated itself to seeking long-term solutions to the evolving demands of its market. Over the last four years, it has invested in developmental projects that will eventually lead to new markets and products.

The 10-K shows five-year trends, which are not always found in annual reports or, if they are, might be chosen selectively. Also included are the amounts paid to each director of the corporation, as well as the names and amounts paid to the five highest-paid officers. If any of the principals are related—personally or through other business ventures—this is also explained. The 10-K financial information must be in audited form. This is not required for the quarterly 10-Q report, however.

Another report of interest to every potential investor is the 8-K, which is a summary of material changes or events. This report must be filed with the SEC within 15 days after the event or change occurs. Typically, the 8-K will include changes in controlling interest in the company, bankruptcy, changes in the company's auditing firm, acquisition of new companies or assets, or the resignation of a director.

To get a copy of any of a company's SEC filings, write directly to the company and request it. The company is required to supply these reports without assessing a fee. If your stockbroker recommends a company, he should give you its 10-K. A competent broker will have seen the report before making any recommendation and will be able to supply you with a photocopy.

If you are considering buying stock in a newly formed company, you will not have an annual report to review, and any filings with the SEC will be preliminary at best. And if you are thinking of buying into an investment other than stock, you might not be able to find as much detailed information as you would like. In these cases, you should always read a prospectus thoroughly before investing any money. This is the subject of the next chapter.

5

THE PROSCPECTUS

Obviously, a man's judgment cannot be better than the information on which he has based it.

Arthur Hays Sulzberger

The Securities Act of 1933 set forth rules of disclosure for a company's prospectus. This law was intended to protect investors by requiring that all risks, fees charged, and qualifications of management be listed. But how complete is the prospectus in spite of these rules, and what good does it do if no one reads it?

A prospectus in a new offering is an abbreviated version of the full registration statement filed with the SEC. Under provisions of SEC Rule 430, a preliminary prospectus (called the "red herring" because of the red ink used on the front cover) can be given to customers even before SEC approval.

The prospectus is far from interesting reading—it is usually drawn up by an attorney for the company making an offer of securities and includes disclosures about the individuals who will manage money, the tax and legal risks in a program or stock offering, use of proceeds and fees that will be charged, conflicts of interest for management, history of performance in similar programs, and, in some cases, an estimate of future profits and losses.

THE PROBLEM OF DISCLOSURE

The 1933 Act was well intended. An approved prospectus does include all of the disclosures a sponsor is required to make, and anyone who reads the document will be able to judge management, fees, and risks. The trouble is that very few investors look at the prospectus beyond the first page or two. So while facts about the program may be disclosed, they are rarely discovered. Even stockbrokers and financial planners usually do not read the prospectus.

Example: Ted was a self-employed management consultant. He opened a Keogh retirement account and set up a self-directed plan with his brokerage firm. He then asked his broker to send him a prospectus for any public syndication programs that, in the broker's opinion, would be good investments within the Keogh account. Ted was an unusually diligent man, and he read the three prospectuses the broker sent.

All three were for partnerships designed to pass through depreciation and other tax benefits to investors. Because the programs contained tax benefits from passive income, the prospectus in each case stated clearly that units of the program should not be purchased for qualified plans like Keogh and IRA accounts.

Ted called his broker and asked about these statements. As he suspected, the broker had not bothered to read the documents, and so he did not even realize the programs were unsuitable for Ted's Keogh account.

From this experience, Ted realized several things. First, the broker was not earning his commission by simply sending prospectuses he hadn't read himself. Most investors depend on their brokers for informed advice, and Ted was not getting that. Ted concluded that he was not being well served. He also knew that reading a prospectus was essential if he was to select the right investment for his Keogh account.

That a prospectus exists and has passed the registration requirements does not mean the SEC has somehow assured investors that a program is valid, well managed, or appropriate. Every prospectus has an important disclosure statement on its cover page, and every investor should read it and understand its significance:

> THESE SECURITIES HAVE NOT BEEN APPROVED OR DISAPPROVED BY THE SECURITIES AND EXCHANGE COMMISSION, NOR HAS THE COMMISSION PASSED UPON THE ACCURACY OR ADEQUACY OF THIS PROSPECTUS. ANY REPRESENTATION TO THE CONTRARY IS A CRIMINAL OFFENSE.

THE MUTUAL FUND PROSPECTUS

A prospectus is published for a number of investments, including:

1. New stock offerings.
2. Publicly offered limited partnerships.
3. Private programs (in which case the document is called the "offering circular").
4. Mutual fund and REIT programs.
5. Certain classes of investment, such as options.

The specific information in any prospectus will vary, but the purpose is the same: to inform you as a potential investor about the structure of an investment or class of investment, its fees and risks, and the people who will be managing your money.

The titles of sections in the prospectus will also vary, depending upon the company and the type of offering. As a rule, though, most fund prospectuses will contain sections with the following titles:

1. Cover page
This contains the names of the fund, the SEC-required disclosure statement, the date the prospectus was prepared, and a brief description of the company.

2. Table of contents

3. Summary

This is a statement of the features of the fund, including "investment objectives," such as long-term growth, current income, or a balance between growth and income.

4. History of fund charges and fees

If the fund has been in existence for a number of years, a section will be included that summarizes income, operating expenses, and dividends. A newly formed offering will show only the intended fee structure of the program. Mutual fund prospectuses include historical return graphs, usually showing what you would have earned by depositing a sum of money at some point in the past and reinvesting all dividends.

5. Investment policies

This section explains your choices. You can receive all dividends and capital gains in cash, or you can have them reinvested. Most funds also offer an automatic cash withdrawal program, under which you will receive a check each month or quarter. This section also explains the minimum amount required by the fund for both initial and subsequent investments.

6. Retirement plans

This section explains how Keogh, IRA, and other retirement accounts can invest in the fund. The minimum required investment may be less than that required for individuals.

7. Share redemption

This section spells out how the fund will send money to you when you decide to sell. It might specify that the request must be in writing and that funds will be mailed within seven days from its receipt. It also defines how shares will be valued —for example, as the closing value of shares in the portfolio on the day the redemption request is received.

8. Charges and fees

If a sales load is assessed, this section explains the rates, and identifies a "breakpoint" for you. For example, if you invest between $1000 and $20,000, the fee may be 8.5 percent. If you invest between $20,001 and $50,000, the fee may be reduced to 7.75 percent.

9. Tax status

This section explains the fund's compliance with regulations of the Internal Revenue Code requiring it to distribute no less than 90 percent of its income to investors in order to retain its tax status. A fund is not taxed itself as long as profits are passed through to investors. This section also explains that the fund will send investors a summary of their taxable income each year within 45 days of the year's close.

10. Management and underwriters

This section identifies the companies that distribute and sell shares, including the underwriter, the custodian, and the individuals who act as the board of advisors (those responsible for actually managing funds).

11. Audited financial statements

This section includes the auditor's opinion, a balance sheet, statement of operations, statement of changes in net assets, and notes to the financial statement.

12. Portfolio of investments

This may be part of the prospectus, or it may be a separate document. It shows the companies in which the fund owns stocks or bonds, including the name, number of shares, and market value as of the latest date. The portfolio summary is usually broken down by industry, giving the total percentage of the portfolio invested in each.

13. Application

In the back of the prospectus is an application form to be used for making an initial investment. Here, you specify how you want distributions of dividends and other income handled (You can have it reinvested or paid out to you in cash, for example). You fill in your name, address, and social security number, and attach a check for your initial investment.

Prospectuses may assign different titles to these sections

and may contain several other sections that discuss the fund's policies and investments.

THE LIMITED PARTNERSHIP PROSPECTUS

A mutual fund prospectus will usually disclose all you need to know about the fund's structure and fees. Compared to prospectuses for other forms of investment, it is a fairly straightforward document. Nevertheless, the existence of a prospectus should not lead investors to assume a program has been thoroughly evaluated and even approved. Again, the absolute importance of the disclosure on the front of every prospectus, in capital letters, cannot be overlooked.

A limited partnership program is an investment made by a number of individuals—limited partners—and the general partners. Limited partners enjoy a limited liability and can lose only as much as they have put at risk. The general partners' liability, however, is unlimited. Limited partners do not have a voice in the management of the program and have little or no control over the way the general partners conduct business. Thus, evaluating the general partners and their qualifications should be your highest priority.

The prospectus (for publicly sold partnerships) or offering circular (for private programs) should disclose all of the information you need to make a judgment about the program. In most cases, though, the information is vague and does not answer the questions that should be of greatest interest to you.

If you are considering investing in a limited partnership, you should read the prospectus with great care. It may include alarming disclosures that investors never see—because they do not take 20 or 30 minutes to read through it. For example, in the section on management, you might discover that one of the managers was recently indicted for securities fraud, or that management has absolutely no experience in the industry.

Key sections of the limited partnership prospectus are similar to those in the mutual fund program. In some cases, a partnership prospectus discusses pro forma operations at length and will include historical returns on other, similar programs offered by the same partners.

A word of caution: Reported historical returns are not necessarily accurate. For example, one real estate partnership prospectus indicated that the general partners had offered four previous programs. According to their report, investors in other programs had earned more than 45 percent per year. But those programs were still in effect at the time of the new offering, and their rates of return were based on assumptions about current market value; no independent appraisal had been performed. A large number of partnership programs have paid inflated prices for properties in the past and estimate current worth of those properties on the basis of original assumptions rather than on their *fair* market value.

Numbers can be manipulated so that any desired result can be reported. Be extremely careful in evaluating a limited partnership program. The broker from whom you purchase those shares should be able to answer all questions you have about the program and its management that are not answered by the prospectus. Every brokerage firm offering units in a partnership is required to perform a process called "due diligence," which is an investigation of assumptions the general partners make, the accuracy of claims, and potential conflicts of interest.

Asking the Right Questions

You should be particularly concerned when general partners (also called, collectively, the sponsor) have offered a number of other, similar programs. In some instances, investors in these programs have made a profit in the following way:

1. An initial program purchased property above market value and enjoyed first-year tax breaks.
2. Years later, another program was formed and new investors paid an even higher price to buy the property from investors in the first program.
3. Current values are highly inflated, so that the reported yield is not realistic.

Now the general partners can report an actual profit earned by investors in the first program, but what is not disclosed is that new investors are actually bailing out the previous program by paying an even greater amount for the same overpriced property.

A section of the prospectus called "Conflicts of Interest" might allude to some conflicts among the general partners but will not spell out in enough detail how those conflicts affect you. In addition to carefully reading this section, ask your broker:

1. Will the program purchase properties in which the general partners or their affiliates hold equity interests?
2. Will the program purchase properties in which investors in other programs offered by the general partners hold equity interests?
3. What payments, if any, will be made to the general partners, their relatives, associates or business partners, and for what purposes?
4. Will the program acquire interests of any type in any other programs offered by any of the general partners?
5. Were existing holdings appraised on the basis of estimates, or was an independent appraisal performed?

In addition to being concerned about which properties the program will buy, you must also pay close attention to fees charged. The limited partnership is sold through a network of brokerage firms, and commissions are paid to brokers that range from 8 to 12 percent or more. Other fees may be paid to the general partners or their friends. In one program, the total paid out from investors' money for initial fees was nearly 60 percent of the total amount of money raised.

This might seem blatantly illegal, but, in fact, it may not be. As long as the prospectus discloses all the fees the investor will have to pay, the general partners have not broken the law. There's a difference between illegal and unethical behavior, and you must ask the right questions before deciding if they are guilty of either, or both.

Also make certain that, along with the prospectus, you or your broker has seen:

- ☐ Audited financial statements of the program and the general partners.
- ☐ Explanations of any pending lawsuits against the program or any of the general partners.
- ☐ Copies of independent appraisal reports.
- ☐ Suitability standards.

The question of suitability can be used as a measurement of risk. Suitability standards are set down in the prospectus to explain who will be allowed to invest. Generally, suitability will include minimum requirements of net worth, annual income, or liquid assets. For example, one prospectus for a private real estate partnership states:

> The investor must have no less than $75,000 annual income (excluding income from investments in the partnership); net worth of $125,000 dollars (excluding real estate); and liquid assets of no less than $25,000.

Your financial suitability is only part of the whole picture. You should also have the level of experience and sophistication as an investor that qualifies you for an especially risky investment. If you must tie up a large sum of money for a number of years, you should understand the special risks of that decision. The sponsor is supposed to determine your suitability for an investment, but, as you can imagine, enforcing a standard is more difficult than merely imposing it. Ultimately, it must be up to you to determine your own level of suitability.

You can judge the degree of risk in a program (notably liquidity, diversification, and tax risks) by the complexity of a suitability statement. The higher the requirements for net worth and annual income, for example, the greater the need for "risk tolerance"—your ability to lose money without causing total devastation to your personal finances. So, if you are seeking a conservative, low-risk investment, a complex suitability requirement is probably a sign that the program is not right for you.

One form of risk in limited partnership investing is the lack of control you have after sending in money. You have no voice in management but give the general partners a free hand in using your funds. Absent from many prospectuses is an explanation of how often the general partners report to you. Get an explanation, in writing, describing the contents of reports you will receive and how often you will receive them. You should receive a status report at least once per quarter that explains the total amount of money the program has raised, where money has been invested, and what profits have been earned. Your share of the total should also be broken out and explained.

Many investors have been frustrated to find out that general partners are very cooperative until they get their money, but do not want anyone asking questions once the program is in operation. If you cannot get answers to all of your questions in writing, don't invest. And don't let your broker talk you out of insisting on answers. If you are told, "The prospectus gives all the answers you need," or "They won't answer that question," look somewhere else. Be as thorough as you need to be to assure yourself that the program is legitimate. An honest general partner will not object to this, and your broker should already have most of the answers—if he has performed his due diligence correctly.

FINDING HIDDEN FEES

The most frustrating part of selecting an investment on the basis of a prospectus is understanding the fees you will have to pay. There is rarely a clear, concise statement of all the fees involved, and information on the various types of fees may be scattered throughout the prospectus.

For limited partnerships, the "Use of Proceeds" section is very important. This is an estimate of how investors' money will be spent. For example, out of a total offering of $15 million, perhaps $3 million will go to various fees and organizational costs, and only $12 million will go into the program.

Fees will include:

- ☐ Compensation to brokers and underwriters (more specifically, a sales commission or load).
- ☐ Management fees—amounts charged by the general partners for investing your money.
- ☐ Payments to others. In some limited partnership programs, a number of fees are included with little or no explanation other than such vague descriptions as loan placement fee, organizational charges, property location fee, and so forth. The charges for legal, accounting, and tax advice are also added in. Make sure you know exactly who gets these fees, how much will be paid, and what relationship the recipient has to the general partners. You will discover that it's often the general partners who get the lion's share of these initial organizational costs.

In mutual fund programs, the level of expenses and fees will vary considerably from one program to another. Most people think of fees only as the load charged when they invest money. But there's more. A "load" is the amount taken from each investment you make to pay a salesperson. Typical is the 8.5 percent fee taken out of all money going into a program and then paid to the salespeople who recommended it. Thus, for every $100 you pay, only $92.50 is actually invested.

Proponents of load funds point out that for the fee you are required to pay, you receive professional advice. The selection of one fund over another is made by an experienced stockbroker or financial planner because you do not know which questions to ask on your own. In reality, you will discover that few of the salespeople who solicit business understand the features of investments beyond the commission rate they will receive for convincing you to invest.

Some funds include a load fee and are sold through brokers. Others are no-load and are sold directly by the fund. Historically, both types of funds have performed about equally, so there's no real justification for the argument that professional advice is worth the load. Some brokers attempt to convince customers that load funds will outperform the no-load variety, but that argument has no historical foundation.

Other Types of Fees

Comparing loads is not a simple matter. Some funds charge the traditional front-end load that most of us already know about—you invest $100, and $8.50 is deducted to pay the salesperson. However, today there are a variety of loads funds may charge.

A deferred sales charge, also called the back-end load, assesses a fee when you sell your shares rather than when you buy. It acts as an incentive for you to leave your money in the fund for a longer period of time. The fee is assessed on a declining scale; so if you leave your money in the fund for a long enough time, there will be no back-end load at all. One fund charges a 5 percent load if you withdraw your funds within the first year, but the amount declines by 1 percent per year until, after the fifth year, there's no fee for withdrawing your money.

Some fees are fixed. The "exit fee," for example, is a percentage charge assessed on all withdrawals, regardless of when they occur.

Funds also charge for managing your money. The load, remember, is strictly for compensation of a broker; don't confuse it with the fund's expense charge or management fee. All funds—load and no-load—charge this fee, which is usually expressed as so much per share or per $100 of total assets.

Since 1980, the SEC has allowed funds to charge customers for marketing expenses. This charge is called the 12b-1 fee, and about 40 percent of all mutual funds actually assess it. Some funds, though, include this fee in their total reported management expenses, while others break it out separately. Many funds do not charge the 12b-1 fee at the time the prospectus is prepared, but they may institute it later.

Because you cannot easily find a disclosure about the 12b-1 fee in the prospectus, and because funds may or may not include it with other charges, a comparison is especially difficult. Most investors select mutual funds on the basis of inaccurate criteria such as:

- ☐ Load versus no-load.
- ☐ Historical performance that will not necessarily indicate the future.

☐ Comparisons of management fees, when an additional 12b-1 fee might come into the picture next year.

In January 1988, the SEC adopted a new rule concerning the disclosure of fees in mutual fund prospectuses. Now, all stock and bond funds making claims about past performance must include total returns for the last one, five, and ten years. In addition, all information about performance in the fund must appear in the same size type, so that selective information cannot be unfairly emphasized. This 1988 rule also requires that all funds use the same formula for calculating yield and total return (total return is the yield plus changes in share value), and that the index in the prospectus include a clear reference to all sales, management, and administrative fees, and 12b-1 charges.

Even with clarification of fees, a comparison of load and no-load is far from sufficient to judge the real cost of one fund against another. It's even possible for a load fund to be less expensive than a comparable no-load.

Example: One load fund does not assess a 12b-1 fee and charges a management fee of 55 cents per $100 invested. A comparable no-load fund does assess a 12b-1 fee, which, combined with management expenses, makes a total charge of $2.23 per $100 invested. You have decided to invest $1000 and plan to leave that amount on deposit for many years.

Your initial evaluation makes the no-load fund seem more attractive because your entire $1000 will be invested. In comparison, the load fund charges you $85 of your $1000, so only $915 actually goes into the fund. But if you compare results over time, you will discover that within six years, the no-load fund is more expensive.

Figure 5-1 shows how the two funds do over six years, assuming that each yields 15 percent per year and that all earnings are reinvested. After the fees are taken out, the no-load fund has a value of $2020.33 and the load fund has a value of $2047.55. The longer the comparison is carried out, the greater the gap in net returns becomes.

YEAR	NO-LOAD FUND PLUS 15%	LESS $2.23 PER $100	ENDING VALUE
1	$1,150.00	$25.65	$1,000.00 / 1,124.35
2	1,293.00	28.83	1,264.17
3	1,453.80	32.42	1,421.38
4	1,634.59	36.45	1,598.14
5	1,837.86	40.98	1,796.88
6	2,066.41	46.08	2,020.33

YEAR	LOAD FUND PLUS 15%	LESS 55 CTS PER $100	ENDING VALUE
1	$1,052.25	$ 5.79	$ 915.00 / 1,046.46
2	1,203.43	6.62	1,196.81
3	1,376.33	7.57	1,368.76
4	1,574.07	8.66	1,565.41
5	1,800.22	9.90	1,790.32
6	2,058.87	11.32	2,047.55

Figure 5-1. No-Load and Load Costs

MAKING AN INFORMED DECISION

Whether you are comparing mutual funds, limited partnerships, or any other form of investment, you can make the right decision only after validating the information at hand. Different programs might make the same argument, but it won't always mean the same thing. A program that includes a 12b-1 charge in its management fee (compared to another program that reports it separately) is one example of this problem.

The prospectus should be reviewed carefully to determine some important answers. If you work with a broker, he should know the answers; however, in the real world, most brokers will not. They will either have to ask their own research department or write to the sponsor of the program.

Obviously, even when you read a prospectus from cover to cover, it will only answer some of the questions you should ask; the document is useful only to a degree. You must also ask questions that the company or general partner is not required to answer in the prospectus but that you need to have answered in order to make the right decision.

Some points to keep in mind:

1. Most brokers have not read the prospectus and do not readily have the answers to your questions.
2. You should always read and understand the prospectus before investing money.
3. You should never invest under pressure. Get answers to *all* of your questions before you make a decision.
4. You should never accept a broker's claim that the prospectus contains everything you need. That's just not true.
5. The fee structure in mutual funds and limited partnerships is rarely simple and requires a lot of questioning. To make a valid comparison, you must first find out about all the fees charged.

Good brokers will educate their customers, and they will perform the valuable service of evaluating and comparing companies and then recommending appropriate investments. Even with the best broker, however, you must be willing to ask questions and wait for answers. The prospectus is an important part of your research, but it does not have all of the answers, either.

A broker might even go so far as to teach you what questions you should ask, which might help you to eliminate 90 percent of the issues you must decide to make the best investment. But that other 10 percent might be the very issues that make the real difference between the best or worst investment choice.

6

INVESTMENT ADVISORY LETTERS

The advantage of doing one's praising for oneself is that one can lay it on so thick and exactly in the right places.

Samuel Butler

The stock market crash of October 1987 took most investors by surprise. But some astute observers realized beforehand that the rapid increases in value would lead to a major retreat. A few newsletter editors predicted the crash very specifically, and those investors who took their advice were not caught unaware.

"Market Brief," published by David P. Luciano (Box 1442, Palmer Square, Princeton, NJ 08542) warned on September 11, 1987:

> The Dow Jones Industrial Average is now catching up with the downtrend of the general market.[1]

And on September 25, 1987:

> The main trend of the market is still negative. It is going much, much lower. It is not yet time to buy stocks.[2]

---

1. "Market Brief," September 11, 1987.

2. "Market Brief," September 25, 1987.

Finally, on October 9, when the DJIA was at 2482:

> The Dow peaked in the middle of August. The long-term uptrend turned down. The downtrend has not yet ended. Major stocks should have been sold. It is not yet time to invest again.[3]

Another accurate predictor of the 1987 crash was Charles Allmon, publisher of "Growth Stock Outlook." The *New York Times*, in an article by John C. Boland, quoted Allmon on August 23, 1987:

> This market has so much froth in it, we're going to have a pretty violent correction. My guess is that we're in the 35 to 50 percent range on the downside.[4]

In both cases, the predictions were right. In hindsight, we can appreciate these observers' amazing accuracy. However, no one has been able to consistently predict the market's future.

Investment advisory letters and forecasting publications offer a variety of views. The best way to decide which ones to follow is to examine the premises on which their advice and conclusions are based, and then select two or three publications that make sense and appear to match your point of view on analysis.

Points of view do vary widely. Some newsletters depend strictly on narrowly focused technical or fundamental indicators and trends. Others have a very broad focus, reporting on a number of different factors and leaving them to the subscriber to interpret.

If you subscribe to a newsletter, remember these important points:

1. There is no inside track on the market. By the time you read something in a published report, hundreds—perhaps thousands—of other subscribers have seen it, too.

---

3. "Market Brief," October 9, 1987.

4. John C. Boland, "A Money Manager on the Sidelines," *New York Times*, August 23, 1987.

2. A past track record might imply a sound principle of management, and it might be self-serving. Don't forget that hindsight is always good.
3. Offbeat formulas will not ensure market success, any more than reading tea leaves can point you to the right stock.

PREDICTION TECHNIQUES

No one method for selecting stocks will ensure success consistently. Even the well-accepted fundamental and technical analysis tools most investors use are not as dependable as many people would like to believe. If you plan to succeed as an investor, you must be willing to research, compare, and take risks. That's a reality every successful investor lives with. If someone did come up with a technique for consistently predicting market movements, it would be well known. It would also revolutionize the way we all invest because it would be a first: the accurate prediction of a random and unpredictable market.

There is a more fundamental reason that accurate prediction is impossible. The market is a supply and demand auction, and the popularity of a stock is based on the collective perceptions of value among investors. If everyone believes a company's stock is going to rise, everyone will buy—and the price will rise in response. It's not that those people were accurate in their predictions; it's just that enough people held the same belief at the same time. And if a stock or an industry falls out of favor with investors, there will be more sellers than buyers. That, in turn, causes the stock to fall in value.

Movement in market price is based on perceptions of value, whether those perceptions are based on technical or fundamental trends or on the collective advice of market analysts. To believe otherwise is pure superstition.

Of greatest value to serious investors are the newsletters that offer the benefits of in-depth and wide-ranging analysis and research. Rather than spend many hours phoning and mailing for information, subscribers use the services of a full-time professional. These newsletters identify companies whose stock has potential for long-term or short-term gains, or comment on the overall trends in the market. They explain the reasoning behind their conclusions, which is as valuable as the conclusions because in doing so they identify first premises. Thus, you can determine whether a particular newsletter conforms to your own philosophy about how to select stocks.

Besides giving subscribers information about promising future investments and emerging trends, the more valuable newsletters also warn investors about negative trends, advising when to sell stocks and even indicating buy and sell ranges.

"Value Line Investment Survey" is probably the most worthwhile research subscription service. The methods it uses to track and rate 1700 stocks are well explained, which enables you to attach degrees of importance to each indicator on the basis of your own beliefs. The weight you give to the Value Line indicators will depend on the definitions you arrive at during your risk and selection process.

Value Line defines its timeliness rankings from 1 (highest) to 5 (lowest). A 1 ranking indicates that a stock is likely to outperform the other 1699 stocks during the coming 12 months. A 3, or average ranking, indicates that the stock will likely perform at the average of the market.

The safety ranking is also defined from 1 (safest) to 5 (greatest risks). Value Line defines safety in a stock's price as the combination of price stability and financial strength of the company. Thus, a stock ranked 5 for safety will be more volatile than the average stock. In a market where prices are depressed, volatile stocks are greater risks but will also outperform the average market on the way up. The opposite will often be true when market prices are excessively high. The lower-ranked stocks will tend to drop at a faster rate than the average.

A safety ranking cannot be considered conclusively as good or bad. Too much depends on timing, current market conditions, and your personal attitude toward risk and potential for future gain.

Timeliness and safety rankings are applied to all of the 1700 stocks in the survey. One full page is devoted to the analysis of each stock. The entire survey is divided into 13 sections, and one section is updated each week.

In addition to the detailed narratives, ratings, and comments about each company, Value Line also sends subscribers a weekly report called "Selection and Opinion," in which present stock market conditions are described and one stock is highlighted. Also in this report, a column is dedicated each week to analysis of certain stock groupings. One week, for example, the report covered stocks with A+ financial strength ratings (separate from timeliness and safety); another week, it dealt with timely stocks with high returns on equity. Major insider transactions and a "Market Monitor" section complete the "Selection and Opinion."

The "Summary and Index," also updated each week, reports on major industries and grouped performance rankings, and on stocks that moved up or down in rank, along with the reasons for the change. It also provides a complete alphabetical list of all 1700 stocks, including rankings and updated results for each, and a number of useful listings. These listings include:

- ☐ Stocks with a ranking of 1
- ☐ Stocks with high 3- to 5-year appreciation potential
- ☐ Cash flow generating stocks
- ☐ Best and worst performers
- ☐ Stocks with widest discounts from book value
- ☐ Lowest and highest P/E stocks

Value Line provides a broad range of updated information and indicators, without advising subscribers on which formula to use. You can select a single factor or any combination of factors you desire in making your selection, and the survey enables you to find what you need quickly.

Standard & Poor's Corporation offers a research subscription service that includes a weekly newsletter called "The Outlook." A subscription includes a copy of the latest *Stock Market Encyclopedia*, which is a compilation of summaries for each stock included in the Standard & Poor's 500 Index.

This service does not offer the in-depth summaries that Value Line provides; however, investors interested in a limited number of selection criteria might find Standard & Poor's to be adequate for their purpose.

Either service can be reviewed on a limited-trial basis. The cost of an initial subscription is fairly low, and if you decide to continue beyond the trial period, most services will apply your payment to the larger annual charge.

Investment advisers, including publishers of newsletters dealing with securities, must obey the law and follow rules established and enforced by the SEC. First, they cannot promise that any one method of selecting investments is guaranteed to succeed or that a particular investment will be a profitable one. They may recommend and support what they say with market signals, but they cannot claim to have a sure thing.

Newsletter editors must also not disclose any inside information they discover. For example, if in the course of research, an editor finds out that a company is about to be taken over, that information cannot be published until the news is made public by the company. And no recommendation can be made based on what the editor learns. It is also illegal for the editor to buy shares in the company on the basis of a tip not known to the general public.

The securities laws also deal with manipulation. Newsletter editors must be careful not to publish any information that would unfairly influence the price of securities to their direct benefit. For example, it would be improper for an editor to make a buy recommendation on a stock in which he owns shares.

Editors can themselves be manipulated by an outside source.

Example: An individual employed by a publicly listed corporation owns several thousand shares of stock and wants to sell. He calls the editor of a newsletter and hints that a new product is about to be announced. In fact, this "hot tip" is false, but the editor recommends the stock, and thousands of subscribers buy it. As a result, the price rises and the individual who made the call sells at a profit. The newsletter editor has a direct responsibility to look out for and avoid this situation.

While many newsletters deal with individual stocks, others concentrate on only one segment of the market. You can subscribe to publications dealing with options, conservative growth stocks, mutual funds, precious metals, takeover candidates, penny stocks, and single industries.

Others offer advice based on a single fundamental or—more often—technical indicator, such as the moves of successful traders, volume analysis, trends in short selling, insider buy and sell activity, chart patterns, price/earnings ratios, income and dividend figures, industry competition, or contrarian investing. These indicators can be very useful, but they narrowly focus on only one aspect among many. Resist following advice based only on one indicator or technique. Try to broaden the sources and types of investment information and advice you receive.

Yet another information source is the compilations of research from other sources. Some newsletters summarize institutional research reports, advice given in market publications, and stocks recommended by various experts. There are even newsletters that report what other newsletters are suggesting.

You cannot tell how useful a newsletter will be until you have seen a copy. Before you subscribe, write to the publisher for a sample copy. Most will gladly send one to you, realizing that the product should sell itself. Avoid any publication that claims it cannot reveal its secrets except to subscribers or that, for any other reason, will not send you a free sample.

Just as researching a company is important before you invest, so is comparing research sources before you subscribe. The annual subscription prices will vary, but can run into hundreds of dollars per year for a weekly or monthly report. That's a lot to pay for four to eight pages of information.

You will discover upon receiving a sample copy that newsletters employ a variety of styles. Some are primarily narrative, analyzing a company, a segment of the market, or a trading technique in some detail. If you are seeking only information, this will be the best kind of subscription for you. Others are very technical and include charts, lists, formulae, and trend analyses involving a lot of math and often complex comparisons. If you appreciate the trending approach and follow it yourself, this will be the most advantageous newsletter subscription for you.

Some newsletters and research services have been accurate most of the time in the past, but none can claim absolute consistency. The *Hulbert Financial Digest* (643 S. Carolina Ave., S.E., Washington DC 20003, 202-546-2164), published by Mark Hulbert, rates the accuracy of predictions, ratings, and recommendations made by newsletters and research services. If you are looking for the service with the best record, a subscription to the Hulbert publication is the best place to start your search.

A 1987 survey by Hulbert compared the results of 10 of the largest services (in terms of total subscriptions). Stock recommendations for a theoretical portfolio were rated from A (in the top fifth) to F (in the bottom fifth). The survey also reported total returns that would have been earned from 1982 through 1986 on the basis of recommendations the newsletters or research services made.

At the top for total return were "Value Line Investment Survey" (169.3 percent); "Market Logic" (140.7 percent); and "Growth Stock Outlook" (128.6 percent). "Value Line" and "Market Logic" were rated A in three of the five years.

Also studied in the survey were "Dow Theory Forecasts" (110.7 percent); "Zweig Forecast" (104.4 percent); "The Outlook" (99.5 percent); "Telephone Switch Newsletter" (74.8 percent); "United Business Service" (43.4 percent); "Professional Tape Reader" (−3.6 percent); and "Granville Market Letter" (−63.9 percent).

None of the 10 services was right every year. You will not find a service that is consistently right. However, there are a few that are on the money most of the time.

CREDENTIALS AND THEIR VALUE

Be sure you understand what you are seeking before you begin comparing newsletters. Some people want pure information—which stocks sell at or below book value, the strongest industries in which to invest, the best option stocks, and so forth. Others want specific advice—What should you buy, hold, or sell now, and why.

Combine an understanding of approach and content. The approach is either sound (based on trends and facts within the market itself) or based on formula (claiming to have secrets for predicting the future). Content is either informative or analytical.

Another factor to consider in choosing a research service or newsletter is the publisher. You can buy either from a recognized research organization or from someone unknown to you. The advantage of the former is that research is gathered and presented consistently. The organization has a well-understood approach, presents its facts in a format that works, and has the resources to provide in-depth information. You cannot always assume this about less well known publishers.

You will gain insights about the newsletter industry by accumulating free samples. Write to publishers for a free recent issue. It might be most revealing to ask for an issue published immediately before a major market event (like the crash of 1987). Also ask these questions:

1. What are your research sources?
2. What fundamental or technical principles do you follow in formulating advice?
3. Do you make specific recommendations?
4. Do you attempt to predict future trends in the market? If so, what method do you use?
5. Can you supply specific examples of past advice and the outcome of that advice?
6. How many months or years have you been offering your newsletter?
7. What is your own background, or the background of your writers and researchers?
8. What comments have been made about your publication's quality? Can you supply copies of reviews?

For a small charge you can obtain a sample package of many different newsletters from companies advertising in investment magazines and newspapers. One company, Select Information Exchange (SIE) (2095 Broadway, New York, NY 10023), offers copies of 20 newsletters of your choice, selected from a list of about 200. They also offer other packages, such as selections of the most popular, most successful, or most comprehensive subscriptions. According to its ad, SIE's range of samples covers publications that cost between $4 and $780 per year. The onetime subscription entitles you to between 1 and 5 copies of each of the newsletters you want to see.

Sending in the small amount of money charged by a referral service like SIE will expose you to a large number of publications. And that is very helpful. But getting copies of newsletters is not the only result. Your name will go onto several mailing lists, which means you can expect the following:

1. You will receive solicitations from many newsletters beyond those you wanted to review.
2. You will receive offers for an assortment of other services —subscriptions, investment opportunities, and magazines, for example.
3. Sample newsletters sent to you will include promotional material. The publishers not only want you to see what they offer; they want to sign you up.

KEEPING IT IN CONTEXT

Recognize newsletters and subscription services as *part* of your investigation. You should not depend on any one source, but instead explore all avenues for dependable information. That means reading prospectuses, examining annual reports and filings with the SEC, using subscription research services, listening to the advice of an experienced broker, and—if you find one you like—studying the information found in a newsletter.

Avoid magic formulas, well-protected secrets, and any form of advice that attempts to tie unrelated factors into the market. The weather probably will affect next year's orange harvest, but it won't directly influence the prices of stocks in the Dow Jones Industrials. And, certainly, short-term movements in prices will not be affected by ice buildup at the South Pole or the thickness of tree rings.

Some indicators not directly related to stock prices might prove valuable, especially if they have ramifications for the economy. Election-year trends are taken seriously by many investors.

For example, one study points to the fact that about 80 percent of the time, the stock market is likely to rise during the fourth quarter of an election year. Whether that is helpful in the future is questionable. The point is that, through their policies and philosophy, individuals voted into office can and do have an impact on the economy—if not by direct action, then at least by the perception of what that impact could mean in the future.

Many indicators can be dismissed with little thought because any reasonably intelligent person will know at once that there is simply no connection. Other indicators can have a temporary or indirect effect on the trend in market prices. For consistent success as an investor, you must regard all sources of information in context. Investigation is the key, and to gain real knowledge and market insight, you must combine what you know and believe with the information you receive from others.

7

FINANCIAL NEWSPAPERS

The trouble with research is that it tells you what people were thinking about yesterday, not tomorrow. It's like driving a car using a rearview mirror.

Bernard Loomis

A trend is useless if you discover its significance only after it has become apparent to everyone else. Looking back at the obvious signs from last year or even last week is of no value. You must be able to interpret what's evolving today and then apply that knowledge through informed action.

You may decide to use fundamental or technical analysis, or both, as part of your total research into investment alternatives. If analysis is to be of any help, though, you must be able to follow the trends on a regular, updated basis. Invariably, this means subscribing to a comprehensive, financial daily newspaper.

Keep in mind that there are dangers in depending too much on daily price changes of individual issues. No matter what your original intention in subscribing to a financial daily, don't fall into the trap of ignoring overall trends and responding only to what's happening from day to day.

This chapter describes the benefits of two major daily papers and compares them. And it suggests guidelines for avoiding problems and making daily information most useful.

A handful of newspapers are designed just for the investor. They summarize most of the popular technical indicators and provide updated fundamental information. Compared with other means of obtaining market data, a financial newspaper offers many advantages:

1. Magazines are more in-depth than daily papers, and report on more narrowly focused subjects. Nevertheless, from the time an article is developed to the date the magazine appears on the stands, two to six months have elapsed. Thus, information and advice are chronically out of date.
2. The financial pages of nonfinancial newspapers are generally brief and incomplete, lacking the scope and depth you seek. For example, many smaller daily papers list New York Stock Exchange prices at midday in order to meet daily printing deadlines. This information, by and large, is of little value.
3. Newsletters and research service publications are not current; they represent weekly or monthly retrospectives on what has already occurred. Also, many newsletters are slanted to reflect a particular point of view.
4. Brokerage research, by the time it gets to you, is no longer current. A report might have been published many weeks, even months, before you see it. In addition, many brokerage firms recommend specific stocks not necessarily because the timing is right but because the firms are committed to selling the shares of that company.

THE MAJOR INFORMATION SOURCES

The *Wall Street Journal* is the most widely used and read financial newspaper. More than four million subscribers receive a complete daily summary of the previous day's news and markets, five days per week.

Perhaps the *Wall Street Journal*'s only flaw is that it contains much more information than many people need. If you only want to review each day's closing prices for your portfolio and read any significant news about companies in which you invest, you will not get maximum benefit from the *Journal*. But if you recognize the need for keeping up to date with the major trends, indicators, and economic news of the day, it is the best subscription for you.

You will not find a more comprehensive summary of news and indicators in any other newspaper. In addition to reporting on strictly financial information, the *Journal* also summarizes major news stories and explains how they affect the markets. Weekly columns summarize trends in small business (Monday), regional perspectives (Tuesday), real estate (Wednesday), marketing (Thursday), and technology (Friday).

Complete daily listings appear for stocks listed on the New York and other major exchanges. Up-to-date listings of options, bonds, and commodity futures are given as well. The *Journal* includes mutual fund quotations, money market rates, foreign exchange rates, dividend news, and summaries of the most widely used technical indicators.

The listings for the New York Stock Exchange include each day's results in these categories:

- Fifty-two-week high and low price, which enables you to measure volatility and also tell whether the current price is near its 12-month high or low.
- Dividend rate, an important factor in the overall rate of return you can expect from a stock investment.
- Price/Earnings ratio—a comparison of current price to annual earnings.
- Volume—each day's trading in shares. Significant volume increases indicate either growing interest in the stock or a large sell-off.
- High, low, and close—the trading range for each day.
- Net price change—the number of points each share rose or fell for the day.

The *Journal* is published by Dow Jones and Company, which also publishes *Barron's National Business and Financial Weekly*. *Barron's* is published every Monday and reports on the previous week in great detail using comprehensive financial tables. It also includes many features and news stories for professional and individual investors.

A free guide to reading and using the *Wall Street Journal* is available from Dow Jones. Both the *Journal* and *Barron's* are published at 200 Liberty Street, New York, NY 10281. The subscription address is 200 Burnett Road, Chicopee, MA 01021, and you can get information on both papers by calling 800-257-1200 (800-222-3380 in Pennsylvania).

Another financial newspaper worthy of serious consideration is *Investor's Daily*. This paper, though smaller in size and scope than the *Wall Street Journal*, offers some features that *Journal* readers do not enjoy. For example, *Investor's Daily* makes it easier to locate significant movement in stocks quickly by a scan of the daily listings. Any stock that rises one point or more or that reaches a new high for the year is listed in bold print. And any stock that falls a point or more or that reaches a new low for the year is underlined.

Like the *Journal*, *Investor's Daily* lists each stock's 52-week high and low price; P/E ratio; volume; high, low, and close for the day; and the point change. But it adds three more features:

1. Earnings per share (EPS) ranking

The EPS ranking is a measure of each stock's growth during the last five years. Stocks are rated from 0 to 99. A high ranking—80 or better—shows a superior EPS record; an 80 tells you that the earnings per share were in the top 20 percent of all listed companies.

2. Relative price strength

This measurement—also ranging from 0 to 99—tells how stable a stock's price has been during the last 12 months. A high ranking indicates that, relative to the market, the price change has exceeded the average. So in an up market, a highly ranked stock exceeded the average price rise. If the market fell, a high ranking indicates the stock's price deterioration was less severe than the average.

3. Volume percentage change

This shows each day's increase or decrease in average volume, compared to the last 50 trading days. When the percentage is +175, for example, that means the volume was 175 percent higher than average for that issue.

These additional features make it easier for investors to track their stocks and identify important changes in market value and perception. They also aid the search for viable investments by adding to the number of possible indicators investors might find useful.

As an example of how these statistical facts can be used, consider an investor who chooses stocks based on an exhaustive collection of information from many sources. His research standards include:

- ☐ Review limited to specific industries that, in his opinion, hold promise for significant growth.
- ☐ Measurements of financial strength.
- ☐ Safety and timeliness ratings assigned by Value Line.
- ☐ Consistent growth in the rate of dividends paid over the last five years.

By applying these standards, the investor is able to eliminate a large number of companies. He also sends away for annual reports and SEC filings, and asks his broker for research reports. Finally, he narrows the field by looking for companies with high earnings per share and relative price strength ratings, according to the *Investor's Daily* listings.

No matter how thorough your investigation, none of the tests you apply to stocks and other investments will ensure success; there is always a degree of risk in picking one investment over another. But with thousands of investments to choose from, having daily statistics helps in the search. In many respects, picking a stock is more a process of elimination than of compiling a list of candidates.

The stock listings in *Investor's Daily* are very useful, especially for a quick review. Each day's paper includes detailed charts for technical analysis, summaries of fundamental and technical indicators, news articles, listings of all issues traded on the major stock exchanges, earnings reports, options listings, mutual funds, commodities futures, bonds, and interest rate figures.

New subscribers receive a reader's guide and a videotape explaining how to use the paper. For more information, contact *Investor's Daily* at P.O. Box 25970, Los Angeles, CA 90025, or call at 800-831-2525 (800-621-7863 in California).

FINANCIAL MAGAZINES

Although daily financial newspapers provide current information in a highly summarized form, more in-depth information will be found in a number of financial magazines. *Fortune, Forbes, Business Week,* and *Financial World* are among the most widely read and respected magazines dealing with big business and investment. They report on trends in major industries and the national and international economy. For example, investors may consider buying stocks in the computer industry because one or more of the magazines have pointed out an emerging trend for increasing demand and lower costs of production.

Magazines report on demographic trends by region and future prospects for specific industries, and they provide in-depth commentary on and analysis of a single company, of a business sector, or of the impact on business strength of political events. This information is valuable for keeping in touch with the general mood of the market, as well as with trends in one company or industry, or in the economy.

Example: A magazine article reports that in one region of the country, a recessionary period is coming to an end. Businesses are increasing their activity there, hiring people, and investing money in new plants and office space. The article concentrates on the major competitors involved in the region, noting that a shortage of commercial space is a severe problem. You hold stock in a major real estate development firm that is active in the same region. Because economic conditions there are improving, you conclude that real estate development will probably increase in the immediate future. The result: greater profits for the company in which you own stock.

Magazines that concentrate on business trends can be a valuable source of information. Another good source is magazines geared more toward the individual investor. *Changing Times, Sylvia Porter's Personal Finance,* and *Money* are leaders in this field.

These publications all include features about different aspects of investing and financial planning for the individual. Unlike publications that follow big business trends, these help people who are seeking investing techniques and a better grasp of how the market works. They include monthly sections on investments with potential for growth, performance results for the leading mutual funds, and features on how to select and manage a portfolio.

APPLYING INFORMATION

Locating sources of information is not the difficult part of investing. What is difficult is knowing how to apply it to making a profit on your investments. With the sheer volume of daily information available to you, it becomes necessary to narrow down what you consider significant—without limiting your review to the point where you make your decisions in a vacuum.

Newspapers and magazines support the efforts of the long-term investor as well as the speculator. The speculator, willing to take great risks, can key in on a single indicator in the daily papers to develop buy and sell signals. And the more conservative investor can use daily, weekly, and monthly publications to compile a vast amount of various fundamental and technical signs; review other material; and compile information to narrow the risks. The danger—at least the perceived danger—is that today's opportunity will be lost if a decision is not made quickly.

Behind that perception is the belief that opportunities are fleeting and so must be taken at once. Many investors fall into the trap of believing this idea, even though they consider themselves to be moderate or conservative. Another point of view looks at the longer term, in the belief that true opportunity does not come and go on a daily basis.

What, then, is the value of daily review? By using the daily newspapers, you gain insights, spot trends, and read news about industries, the economy, and individual issues. And they also provide you with valuable information you can incorporate into your own investing standard. For example, the *Investor's Daily* listings of EPS and relative price strength can be used as a method of elimination, and a feature about a particular market sector can further narrow the field of review.

Remember, though, that by the time you read about an opportunity, it's too late to take advantage of it. A huge rise in yesterday's market value is worth knowing about only if you bought the stock last week or last month. You must be able to keep today's information in perspective: To a large extent, it is a report of what has already happened. You put this information to the best use when you use it to anticipate what is likely to happen in the immediate future.

Just as fundamental and technical analysis in any form can be a valuable piece of the total puzzle, the collective information in the daily papers adds to your overall knowledge and perception of the market. You can eliminate the hours required to go through every page of a daily paper by restricting what you read to applicable news items, a few selected indicators, and the listing of a few issues you want to follow.

Your investment decision should be a combination of information from many sources. Rather than label yourself as a fundamentalist or technician, use what you consider valid and invest according to the total sum of news and information at your disposal. For example, you might depend on:

1. Technical indicators for the market, industries, and individual stocks shown in the daily papers.
2. Value Line's safety and timeliness rankings and industry evaluations.
3. Comparisons of fundamental trends shown in corporate annual reports and SEC filings.
4. Your broker's research reports.
5. Individual stock criteria:
    - ☐ beta
    - ☐ volatility

- [ ] industry
- [ ] growth in sales
- [ ] charting patterns

A PERSPECTIVE ON TIMING

Depending too heavily on what you read in the daily financial papers and monthly magazines can be a trap. A regular review can easily cloud longer-term judgment about the market. We tend to become impatient if, after we buy 100 shares of stock, it does not rise immediately. After three or four weeks of seeing the stock move by one-eighth of a point or so every day, and only within a one- or two-point range, the question arises, "Why isn't my stock doing anything?"

In fact, a few weeks is not a long time at all; it only seems that way. Impatience can become your worst enemy. You must define your priorities as an investor. Are you looking for extremely short-term profits, or are you in for months or even years?

If you want to speculate, meaning you expect fast profits, you must also be willing to make quick decisions. Perhaps the level of risk that speculators assume is connected more to the quickness of the decision than to anything else. The speculator does not have the time for a detailed, methodical analysis of all the fundamental and technical indicators available, and must narrow the focus to one or two daily bits of information.

If you are interested in long-term growth, meaning you are willing to buy and hold stock for many months or years, you can afford a more methodical approach to investigation. This is where the daily paper can become your best source for ongoing information, or become the worst place to look every day.

Investors should not ignore available information just because they consider themselves permanent stockholders. You certainly owe it to yourself to look for news that affects the stocks you own. For example, the *Wall Street Journal* includes a daily index of stocks in the news. By reading the articles about stock you own (or are considering buying) you keep up with important news—new products, competition, dividends declared, profits reported, litigation, labor relations, plant openings and closings, appointments of new executives—and other pertinent information that affects you and the value of your investment.

Too many investors subscribe to daily papers with the initial idea that they will read all the news of interest to them. They soon find, though, that all they look at on a regular basis is the daily closing price of stock.

For the long-term investor, minor daily price changes hold no immediate interest. At the time you buy, you should set standards for yourself. For example, you bought 500 shares of stock several months ago at $16 per share. You determine that if and when the stock's market value climbs to $25 per share, you will sell. That will yield a profit of $4,500.

If you set a goal like this, are you truly a long-term investor? Not necessarily. What if the stock rises to $25 in a few days? What will you do at that point? You might end up being a relatively short-term investor. There's no fault in realizing a $4,500 gain in a few days, but it also puts you back where you started. You then choose another investment equally worthwhile.

It could be that the stock you buy will rise to your target price quickly. You could sell, and if the stock then falls, you could repurchase. That is a fortunate series of events, but you cannot depend on its occurring with any consistency. Chances are equally good that the stock will continue to rise, meaning you lose out on more opportunity for profit.

Review the daily listings with self-definition in mind. Are you truly a long-term investor, or are you a speculator? Or does your philosophy fall somewhere in between? Knowing who you are will help you to make the best use of daily information.

Avoid defining yourself as a long-term investor and then acting like a speculator. This is the great trap of daily review. If you do intend to hold stock for one or two years or more, look at the price as often as you like, but stick with your original goal. If you bought the stock because you believed its future potential was great, don't sell too soon to take a quick profit. Respect your own goal and your purpose in making the investment.

Keep your investing philosophy in mind whenever you decide to sell. Buying is only the first part of the successful investment equation. All of the careful research you perform to identify the best potential for long-term gains goes out the window if you change your strategy to take short-term profits.

Example: You buy 300 shares of stock at $27 per share because you believe the stock has the potential for substantial growth over the next three years. You intend to hold that stock for no less than 36 months. However, within 4 months after you make your purchase, the stock's value has risen to $35. You sell, taking a profit (before trading commission) of $2,400. A few months later, the stock's market value is above $50 per share.

In this case, you did not follow your original long-term goals after your purchase of stock. You took a limited profit but ignored the recognized potential for growth. You gave up the longer-term growth that first attracted you to the stock, thus violating your standards and discounting the value of your research.

Looking at daily listings adds temptation to the life of the long-term investor. The problem is that, as a stock's value begins to climb, the tendency is to constantly compare it to the basis, or original price paid for it. This is a natural tendency; we all want to know where we stand and how much of a profit we could take by selling our stock today. But it can also be a trap. Rather than ask yourself how much profit you could realize today, ask whether the runup in price is within your own expectations. If you have done your research well, chances are the price rise reflects only the beginning of prosperity for the company.

If you also watch technical indicators, you might look for signals that the stock, its industry, or the overall market is due for a reversal. On the basis of the charting patterns, index signs, and other indicators, you might be better off taking profits while they are there. But, again, this approach makes you a technician and increases the tendency towards short-term investing. This may be contrary to your philosophy that a stock should be held for a set period of time.

The daily papers are the best source for current information, but don't allow the short-term trends they emphasize to alter your longer-term goals and investing standards. Use a combination of fundamental and technical analysis, follow your stocks carefully, and time your purchase and sale decisions. Most important, always operate within the limits of the objectives you have defined for yourself. Successful investors may suffer from daily uncertainties about the market, but they always have their eye on their own, individual target.

8

SEMINARS AND CLASSES

It is not the crook in modern business that we fear, but the honest man who does not know what he is doing.

Owen D. Young

There are good reasons to attend an evening class, or even a seminar or convention on investments. For beginners, the vast number of special terms and phrases can be intimidating and frustrating. A basic introductory course will demystify the language and provide a starting point. And for the more advanced investor, a specialized class in a more focused market segment is a good way to acquire information.

The real knowledge and experience, however, come from actually putting money on the line, as an investor. We only appreciate our real comfort zone once we have money at risk. Nevertheless, education can introduce investment concepts, provide a working knowledge of rules and terms, and teach us how to evaluate risk without actually risking money.

INVESTOR ASSOCIATION MEMBERSHIP

One of the best sources for education and ongoing study is the American Association of Individual Investors (AAII) (625 North Michigan Avenue, Chicago, IL 60611). Investing on your own is a lonely experience, and the continuing education and support provided by AAII's local chapters—not to mention its yearly seminars—can offset the isolation that solitary investors often feel.

The American Association of Individual Investors is a nonprofit organization with approximately 100,000 members and chapters in 43 cities. Formed in 1979, it describes itself as an "educational group for cautious and serious investors."

Benefits of membership include:

- The *AAII Journal*, published 10 times a year, which provides information on investment theory and practice and refers readers to other publications and sources for information.
- The annual *Investor's Guide to No-Load Mutual Funds*, sent free to all members of AAII.
- Membership in a local AAII chapter, which holds periodic meetings featuring speakers on a variety of investment topics.
- An extensive *Year-End Tax Strategy Guide* sent to each member every November.
- Home study programs on all aspects of investing.
- Optional membership in an AAII subgroup of computer users, including a bimonthly newsletter, "Computerized Investing"; a software exchange program; and an electronic bulletin board.
- Discounts on subscriptions to *Forbes, Business Week, Boardroom Reports, Fortune,* and *Bottom Line* magazines, as well as discounted prices on other magazines and investment books.

The association sponsors six different seminars, held yearly in Chicago, Los Angeles, New York, Boston, San Francisco, and either Detroit or Washington DC. Certain of the seminars are also held in four to five additional cities. The six seminars are described below.

1. Investing Fundamentals

Where to get information; how to select, buy, and sell stocks and bonds; basic analysis.

2. Stock Analysis and Portfolio Analysis
Valuation methods; the use of investment models; types of information required.

3. Economic Analysis for Investment Decision Making
An in-depth explanation of the *Wall Street Journal*: what's in it, what it means, how to use it.

4. Introduction to Personal Financial Planning
Basics of financial statements; how to set goals; estate planning; financial management.

5. Mutual Funds and Your Investment Portfolio
How to build a portfolio of funds; types of fees; how to read a fund prospectus.

6. Real Estate Investment Decision Making
Investment through direct ownership of investment property; partnerships, REITs, and other real estate pools; financing and cash flow.

Membership in AAII is worthwhile to beginners as well as more experienced and sophisticated individual investors. Nevertheless, it is not the only source of information offered. You can also find information at free seminars, evening classes, or investment conventions.

THE FREE SEMINAR

A training orientation meeting for newly hired salespeople in one securities brokerage firm includes instructions on organizing evening seminars. The idea behind the seminars, of course, is to bring in as many people as possible, offer them information, and then make a concentrated sales pitch.

From the salesperson's point of view, this is a better way to make contact than cold calling because a seminar audience is there by its own will. The presentation looks informational, but, in fact, it is a form of sales pressure. If applied skillfully, the pressure is subtle enough so that people do not know they are being sold, but this is rare. Most free seminars are blatantly high-pressure affairs.

The free seminar tactic takes advantage of your desire to learn, and it succeeds best when attendees are the least knowledgeable. For you, buying under pressure is the worst way to start out as an investor.

The typical seminar is held at a local meeting room, often in a hotel, and advertised in newspapers or on local radio and television. Sometimes, a target list is available to the salesperson running the meeting, and invitations are mailed out that read something like this:

> **The Path to Wealth in the Coming Decade**
> **A free seminar**
> **By invitation only.**
> **Discover the new investment opportunities**
> **and find out how to protect yourself against**
> **risks while earning double-digit returns in the coming ten years.**
> **R.S.V.P. 555-1122**
> **Tuesday, May 16, 8 p.m.**
> **Downtown Hotel**

Whenever you read or hear an ad for a free seminar, realize that it will be, in fact, nothing more than a sales meeting. You certainly would not respond if the ad told the truth, just as you are unlikely to let someone in your house who comes to sell you insurance or mutual funds. Those problems—from the salesperson's point of view—are eliminated by the free seminar.

A variation of this technique is the offer of a free financial evaluation you receive in the mail from a local insurance agency. This is a method for getting the agent's foot in the door so that he can make a sales pitch, but it sounds like a great deal. The typical announcement reads:

> Your name has been chosen from a carefully screened list. We are offering a free financial evaluation to a select few people who are interested in protecting their future.

To make a no-obligation appointment, please fill in and return the enclosed card.

On the card is space for your name, telephone number, and age. The age is critical, because the agent needs that to determine what your premium will be.

The life or health insurance product he intends to sell you will not come up as the result of a financial evaluation—it is known in advance. The offer is a sales technique, and what is called an evaluation is nothing but a series of arguments to convince you that a particular product is essential to your financial health.

Your free evaluation will consist of one of the following:

1. A free computer-prepared comparison showing how your present policy stacks up against the policy the agent wants you to buy. This is offered as an objective comparison that may show that your present insurance is sufficient. But, invariably, it will prove that the new product is a better buy and offers much more. This is a sales trick, not a true comparison.
2. A financial needs analysis showing how much your family will suffer if you die before your time. The analysis makes many assumptions about future inflation and family budgets so that the conclusion will be alarming, geared to convincing you of the need for a substantial amount of insurance protection.
3. A sales pitch, without any pretense of an educational or free service.

Many firms have gone to great lengths to make their sales pitches look like free offers. One firm has a booth at county fairs and other public gatherings and offers a free drawing. You are asked to fill out a card with your name, address, phone number, and age. The prize is a one-hour free consultation—a $200 value. Of course, everyone who fills out a card wins. You receive a phone call or letter congratulating you on your good fortune. The next step is making an appointment. You are excited about the prize and might not even realize until after the contract has been signed that the entire experience was a clever sales trick.

If you are looking for a broad range of free information, you probably won't find it at an investment convention. Investment conventions are held in different regions of the country, and though purportedly aimed at the consumer, in reality they are great opportunities for salespeople. Although the convention typically offers some 30- to 60-minute presentations that are strictly informative, it is primarily a gathering of salespeople, all of whom want to talk to you.

The disappointing part is that you actually pay to attend—a pass to a convention might cost as much as $200 or more. Literature promotes the convention as educational, but what you see when you arrive is a hall filled with booths, all offering products or consultation, or both. There may be hundreds of such booths lined up in columns. As you walk through seeking information, you soon discover that there's little to be had. And if you stop at a booth to pick up a free brochure (actually sales literature), you will be pressured to fill out the inevitable card.

During the day the convention is held, a number of speakers are usually giving talks in an adjoining meeting room. A few are informative, but most are there to endorse a product or line of products. A speech may provide attendees with the details of investing, including in-depth reporting about the safety of buying real estate or mutual funds or bonds. But when all is said or done, most of them are just lengthy sales pitches.

THE INVESTMENT CLASS

You have a better chance of picking up truly useful information by attending an investment class offered by a local community college. A class is especially worthwhile if you are new to investing and want to learn a lot of the basics in a structured, organized forum. For advanced study of investing, however, you are unlikely to find a class. Once beyond the basics, investors' interests usually become so specialized that an evening class in one type of investing cannot attract enough people to justify offering it. You will find out more by buying a book or subscribing to a service and studying on your own.

Most evening classes cost very little. The registration fee will range between $10 and $50, and books and other materials should cost no more than $25. The class generally meets once a week for 8 to 15 weeks.

Before signing up, find out who the instructor is and what guidelines the college has placed on the material to be covered and the style of teaching. If the instructor is employed by the college, the course will be academic. That means you will receive a lot of theory but very little practical information. You're much better off if the class is taught by someone who deals in the real world on a daily basis. That means a professional in the field.

Now you will be faced with a problem of a different kind. Chances are, if the instructor is a professional in the investment community, she makes a living by selling products and earning a commission, and thus will have a particular point of view about financial services and about how you should invest. This point of view will not always correspond with your best interests.

When you inquire about a class, ask the college representative the following questions:

1. What is the course outline? Can I receive a copy?
2. Who is the instructor, and what does she do for a living?
3. Have you given the instructor guidelines and restrictions about solicitation in the class? (For example, has the college specified that the instructor may not pass out sales literature?)
4. Has the instructor taught this class before?
5. Can you put me in touch with the instructor directly?

You should look for a class taught by a professional in the field, who will be able to tell and show you how successful investors operate—with or without the advice of a financial planner. You might decide later to use a professional's advice, but you certainly don't want to attend a 10-week course that is, essentially, a drawn-out sales presentation.

If the college will not provide you with the instructor's

phone number, leave your number and ask that the instructor get in touch with you. Ask her these questions:

1. What are your objectives in teaching the class? What should I expect to learn from you?
2. What is your philosophy about investing? (For example, does she believe in first gathering knowledge, defining personal goals and risk standards, and so forth? Or does she believe you should trust someone else exclusively?)
3. How long have you been in the investment business? What previous course experience do you have?
4. Can you refer me to someone who has taken this course from you?

As you have probably noticed by now, this is a recommendation for a thorough initial investigation before taking a class. The approach should be familiar: It is the same as the process you will go through to identify the best investments.

What should you expect to gain from attending an investment class? Set goals for yourself and identify what you expect to achieve, such as:

1. An introduction to the fundamental concepts of investment—risk, safety, diversification, liquidity, types of investment products.
2. Methods for developing your own financial goals and risk standards.
3. Planning techniques and guidelines.

OTHER SOURCES

Classes and information are available outside of community colleges. Perhaps the best noncollege source for both is offered by regional chapters of investment associations. The National Association of Investors Corporation (NAIC), for example, helps to educate its members through its regional councils. The format it uses is not the classroom but a combination of materials and information that may be just as valuable. The National Association of Investors Corporation is a nonprofit group serving investment clubs, but it also provides a range of other services and educational materials to its members. Its services are discussed in more detail in the next chapter.

EDUCATION IN PERSPECTIVE

There are no secrets worth learning; there is only the truth. Keep this in mind whenever you are considering a class, seminar, convention, or other source for information.

It would be a mistake to believe that by listening to someone else, you will discover the secrets of investing success. The only way to succeed is by defining standards, gathering current information, and sticking to your own rules. The promise to reveal secrets is yet another sales ploy, often used to lure you to a sales meeting.

Nevertheless, you can learn a great deal by attending the various seminars that are offered. Just be sure you know, going into one, that it is really a sales meeting. By listening carefully, you will gain insight into sales techniques, and you will discover many of the strong and weak points of products.

With that knowledge, you can then decide, on your own, where and when to invest. Information can be either positive or negative. You must know the risks and shortcomings of an investment, as well as its potential for profits, before making a truly informed decision.

Don't avoid seminars just because they are fronts for an hour-long sales pitch. Willingly fill out cards and send them in, and take your free hour of consultation. Attend conventions if you wish, and give your name to all of the salespeople—but just to gather information. Don't buy anything, and don't be swayed by convincing arguments. If you first gather information from all sources and then compare and evaluate, you will make the right decisions on your own.

When you attend a sales convention, go prepared with a list

of questions to ask during the inevitable question-and-answer period. You will discover much more about the product by asking questions than you will from the presentation itself. Your questions should include the following:

1. How long have you been offering programs like this one?
2. Can you make available to investors a track record of past capital raised, profits, and cash flow?
3. What percentage of invested funds actually goes to the investment, and how much will be paid in commissions, fees, and other expenses before the investment is made?
4. What is your commission rate for selling this program?
5. Do you have a prospectus? Does it disclose all payments to general partners and to salespeople, and on what page?
6. Can you supply the names and phone numbers of people who have already invested their money?
7. What licenses do you hold, and how long have you held them?
8. How many years have you been in this business, and in your current capacity?
9. Can I have copies of all your literature to show my financial advisor before I make a decision?

If the presenter evades answering *any* of these questions, you can conclude that there's something to hide. Either he has no experience or qualifications, or the program has weaknesses that—from his point of view—are better left unrevealed. You and the others attending the meeting will see from these questions just how well the presenter understands the product. Often, you will see that this supposed expert really knows very little beyond a few highlights from the sales literature and how to fill out an application form.

The questions above are entirely proper and should always be asked by anyone thinking about investing. Yet few salespeople will gladly answer them. Even when there's nothing to hide, the issues these questions raise are simply not positive selling points.

By joining AAII and seeking out valid, useful educational

outlets through your local college and financial planning community, you can establish a strong base of knowledge. Beyond that, you can benefit from the combined research capabilities of other investors by joining or forming an investment club. That is the topic of the next chapter.

9

INVESTMENT CLUBS

Help me to money and I'll help myself to friends.

Thomas Fuller

As an individual investor, you work in isolation. Even when you send away for information, contact a broker every day, and speak with other investors, you're still all alone when you make that decision to buy or sell.

In something as important as managing money, it is always desirable to share decisions with other people. As a solitary investor, you compete with institutions—pension plans, mutual funds, insurance companies, and other investing groups—that have huge amounts of money to invest, giving them flexibility in the market. And they have their own research facilities and staffs. You have no one but yourself.

You can get around this problem by delegating responsibility for your investing decisions. The most popular way to do this is by buying shares in mutual funds and other pools. However, if you like the idea of directly managing your money, a mutual fund is not the answer. The solution is to join or start an investment club—a group of individuals like yourself who band together and invest as a single unit. Profits—or losses—are shared by all members.

THE VALUE OF INVESTING WITH OTHERS

The investment club is a simple but very effective way to invest. Each member (there are usually between 5 and 15 people) puts in the same amount of money each month, and the pool is managed and invested as a single unit. The decisions on what to buy and when to sell are made by the group on the basis of collective research and an agreed-upon standard for risk and safety levels.

If this sounds like a mutual fund, that's exactly what it is, only on a smaller scale. But as one of the owners, you are involved directly in the decisions that the club makes as a whole.

There are four strong arguments for joining an investment club:

1. Varied backgrounds

An investment club is more than just a vehicle for pooling money; it is also a social event, for which several people get together each month. The clubs that succeed are composed of people who have something in common. Similarities in economic status, jobs and interest, age, investing philosophy, and education are all important elements in making the club an enjoyable and satisfying experience.

However similar the club members are, though, they represent a variety of life experiences. This is an advantage to the collective membership. When you add together the knowledge and experience of 10 or more people and put it to work toward one purpose, you have a powerful bank of information at hand.

2. Flexibility

An individual who can afford to invest $100 per month has a limited range of choices in the market. But if 10 people each put in that amount, the total fund is $12,000 per year.

Flexibility means the ability to diversify—an essential principle of smart investing. You need to plan a portfolio that spreads risks among several dissimilar investments, so that no one adverse factor will destroy your investing plan. A single investor, unable to afford true diversification, often turns to a mutual fund. In an investment club, you and your fellow members enjoy greater flexibility and diversification than any single investor could.

3. Education

Participation in an investment club is an educational experience. You gain personal knowledge as an investor just by participating in the decision process. You also benefit by working with a group, observing its actions, and listening to its suggestions.

Because you will be working with a much larger resource pool, you also find out about a variety of investment alternatives. If you want to learn about how to succeed in the market, the investment club might be the fastest and most economical way to get started.

4. Shared research

You already appreciate the importance of thorough research, but by now, you probably have also concluded that investing makes great demands on your time. Wading through research reports, newsletters, magazines, financial statements, and books requires a lot of time, and absorbing everything you read is no easy task. In a club, the responsibility for gathering and digesting information is shared.

For example, if each of 15 members spends three hours each week in research, that's a total of 45 hours. If you had to do that much investigation on your own, it would be a full-time job.

Figure 9-1 summarizes the advantages of an investment club.

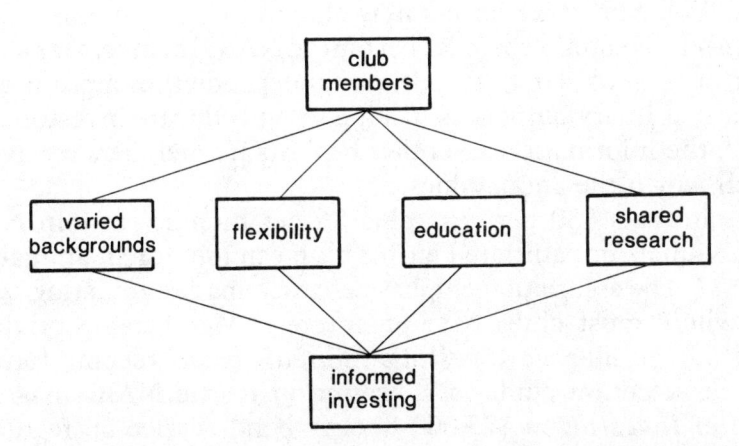

Figure 9-1. Advantages of Investment Clubs

SOME IMPRESSIVE STATISTICS

Investment clubs have been active in the United States since about 1900. Since then, successful clubs (i.e., those that remain active) have outperformed the market *and* most professional money managers.

Many newly formed clubs do not last beyond the first year. Like any collective effort, success depends on a common and agreed-upon cause and the active participation of everyone involved. If conflicts arise, members lose interest and the club dissolves. Those clubs that last, however, prove to be very worthwhile for their members.

The National Association of Investors Corporation (NAIC), a nonprofit association for investment clubs and their members, reports that their clubs have outperformed the Standard & Poor's 500 Index in 20 of the last 26 years. And over a 5-year period ending in 1986, they gained 322 percent, compared with a 146 percent increase in the Dow Jones Industrials. The average club, according to an April 1986 NAIC survey, earns 20.3 percent per year on its portfolio.

NAIC clubs normally contain about 15 members, each member investing about $28 per month. About half of all newly formed NAIC clubs are still together 18 months after formation, and after 7 years, the average club's portfolio is worth $65,000. NAIC today has more than 125,000 members in over 7000 clubs.

You can either form a new club or join an established one. New clubs should consider becoming NAIC members for a number of reasons. First, NAIC is an independent, nonprofit group whose primary purpose is to support and educate investors. Second, the information and other benefits its members receive are well worth the annual dues.

It costs $30 per year plus $6 per member to join NAIC. Individuals not affiliated with a club can join for an annual cost of $27. The association emphasizes stock market investing, which is where most clubs have an interest. Membership privileges include an 80-page *Investor's Manual;* recordkeeping forms; a stock selection guide; a subscription to the NAIC magazine, *Better Investing;* a $25,000 fidelity bond; advice on regulatory matters; and participation in regional classes and meetings and an annual national convention. Contact NAIC at 1515 Eleven Mile Road, Royal Oak, MI 48067 (313-543-0612).

SETTING GOALS

For any investor—whether an individual or a group such as an investment club—setting standards and investing goals is a necessary first step. The clubs that dissolve within the first year or two most often do so because members cannot agree on investing standards.

The successful clubs spend considerable time developing their initial goals. One club, for example, might be interested in conservative long-term growth only and will invest according to that standard. Another club might specify that of the total portfolio, 50 percent should be invested in growth, 25 percent in income, and 25 percent in money market funds.

The first thing a club should do is write down the goals and risk standards that will be followed. This should include specific details about how members will set standards for each investment. For example, how will the club decide when to sell a particular investment? A standard must be set in advance to avoid uncertainty and dissent later on.

NAIC suggests that four preliminary standards be agreed to by clubs formed with conservative goals. They are:

1. Invest the same sum of money in the stock market every month, regardless of general market conditions. NAIC supports the idea of dollar cost averaging (average costs are reduced when the same amount is invested and prices change).
2. Always reinvest dividends and capital gains as soon as they are earned to maximize and compound the rate of return.
3. Buy shares of growth stocks—those that offer the potential for greater value in the future. NAIC defines growth stocks as shares of companies whose sales are growing at a rate greater than the industry average.
4. Diversify in several fields to reduce risk and increase opportunities for profit.

When you form a new club, make sure all members agree on investing standards. After a general discussion, appoint two or three members to draft a preliminary statement of investing objectives and risk standards. The following questions should be addressed in this statement:

1. What is the club's primary objective in investing? Do we consider ourselves conservative or aggressive?
2. Do we want to place part of our total portfolio in higher-risk investments? What percentage?
3. How will we decide on purchases?
4. What is the procedure for selling? Will we sell upon reaching a predetermined rate of return? Or, in the event of a loss, will we bail out when a predetermined percentage has been lost?

The successful club also has a clear, written statement of objectives—to which all members agree and stick with. Of course, as the club progresses, the goals might change. In that case, a consensus of the membership is necessary to ratify any changes.

Also essential to a successful club is that all members remain active. That means everyone must agree to invest the same amount each month. Equally important is that everyone share in the research, attend meetings, and vote on investment decisions. To be avoided is the situation where 20 percent of the people do 80 percent of the work.

INITIAL FORMATION

Investment clubs offer obvious benefits to those who are new to investing, through diversification, sharing of risks, and joint research. How do you organize an investment club?

Most clubs are formed as partnerships. As long as 50 percent of the original owners are still involved, individuals can come and go without the partnership having to dissolve. This makes it easy to account for old members leaving and new ones joining, as the group does not have to be reformed with every change in membership.

At the end of each year, a partnership tax return is filed for information purposes. Total profits are broken down so that members can report their share of the total on their individual tax returns. For example, 10 people form an investment club on January 1. Each puts in $30 per month, and the pooled funds are then invested. During the year, the pooled funds earn $710 in profit. As long as all 10 members remain in the club and each one's periodic investment is the same, the profit calculation is a simple one. Each member is assigned $71 in earnings.

The calculation is different, however, if one member leaves during the year. Suppose that after seven months, an individual quits the club. He is paid his initial investment of $210 plus $35 earned to that point. For the balance of the year, the remaining nine members split the profits equally. The calculation for the whole year is broken down this way:

Total Earnings

Member	Months 1–7	Months 7–12	Total
1*	$ 35	$ 0	$ 35
2	35	40	75
3	35	40	75
4	35	40	75
5	35	40	75
6	35	40	75
7	35	40	75
8	35	40	75
9	35	40	75
10	35	40	75
Total	$350	$360	$710

*resigned

Total shares (or, more accurately, units) of the partnership must be similarly adjusted if any members alter the amount they put in each month. For example, a member might miss a monthly contribution, or might want to double her participation.

In the latter case, she will earn twice the amount of those investing the agreed-upon amount. A missed contribution means that the member's proportionate shares will be lower than everyone else's.

Allowing individual members to increase shares should be carefully considered. Clubs generally keep things simple by keeping ownership equal. That way, each person has one vote. If a club ends up with an unequal distribution of power, minority owners will have less of a voice, and the entire concept becomes less practical.

FORMING YOUR OWN CLUB

To start your own investment club, first identify likely members out of your friends or coworkers, and invite between 20 and 25 of them to an initial meeting. Even though you want to limit membership to 15 or fewer people, you should never expect all of those you invite to join up.

NAIC suggests inviting someone from an existing investment club to the first meeting to speak to your group, answer questions, and offer suggestions for getting the club going. NAIC will refer interested people to active clubs in their area.

Once an interested group has gathered, begin by discussing specifics. How much will each person invest per month? When will meetings be held? Who will draft the initial statement of standards and objectives? Who will keep the books? Will the club join NAIC?

One important benefit of joining NAIC that a club in its formative stages should keep in mind is that membership includes a $25,000 fidelity bond. As your club grows, you can purchase additional fidelity protection up to a million dollars.

Although it's possible that one member will misappropriate funds, NAIC reports that, in 30 years, only about 50 cases of theft have been reported out of a total of 45,000 clubs.

Make certain that members understand their responsibilities. Besides agreeing to invest money each month, they should commit to spending a specific amount of time on research so that they will be prepared to make a contribution at the monthly (or weekly) meetings.

The club should agree on which stockbroker or brokerage firm to use. The commission cost is an important consideration in the formation of a club. It could be substantial if members will be trading actively. If the members agree to take a personal role in researching investments, however, the advice of a full-cost broker is probably not necessary. They should consider the savings possible with a discount broker (see Chapter 10).

Once an account is established for the club at a brokerage firm, the members must decide how many of them will be authorized to contact the broker and make investment transactions. It's a wise policy to limit the number to one or two in order to avoid confusion and possible errors in trades.

Many individuals have started out in investing by forming or joining clubs. And even after learning how to devise a strategy and put it into practice, they often remain with the club, in addition to investing on their own. In the beginning, the club can serve as a practical classroom for the novice, and later, it can be an enjoyable and profitable social event.

In the next chapter, the value of a brokerage relationship, discount brokers, and financial planners are discussed.

10

BROKERS AND FINANCIAL PLANNERS

Judgment comes from experience and great judgment comes from bad experience.

Robert Packwood

We all start out wanting to trust other people, especially when we are ourselves inexperienced. This is as true for new investors as it is for beginners in other situations. The problem with trust, for investors, is that not everyone wearing the label of broker, planner, or adviser is trustworthy. Until there is a uniform means of regulating this industry, you have no way to determine in advance whether your adviser is working in your best interests or in his own.

Financial planners are not tested and approved by any regulatory agency in the way that accountants, attorneys, and other professionals are. The states have yet to devise a method for screening advisers and for establishing minimum qualifications. This means that anyone may present herself as a financial planner, and you cannot assume automatically that she possesses any qualifications to advise you.

According to a 1988 survey conducted by the North American Securities Administrators Association (NASAA) and reported by the Associated Press, consumer losses due to fraud in the financial services industry totaled $397 million between 1986 and 1988 (NASAA can be contacted at 202-737-0900). That is only the reported total, representing 79 cases in 30 states that were reported to securities industry regulators. It shows a more than 300 percent increase over reported losses between 1983 and 1985.

There is a complete lack of oversight in this industry. Any company offering advice on securities must register with the SEC as investment advisers, but there are no standards for experience or education. And financial planners who do not give advice on the purchase of securities are not required to register at all. So a planner who offers to prepare a plan for a fee but who does not suggest purchasing particular stocks, bonds, or other securities, is completely free from regulatory jurisdiction.

In a February 1985 study, the SEC reported that 85 percent of all financial planners make money at least in part through commissions. Many represent themselves as independent and claim to be compensated by fees they charge to clients, but, according to the SEC, fewer than half of all planners told their clients they would earn a commission for placement of securities investments.

There are several designations awarded to qualified financial planners. Those who have earned some of these designations have at least established their exposure to financial information. That exposure, combined with several years of experience, qualifies an individual to work as a financial planner.

First is the securities license, which is granted by the National Association of Securities Dealers (NASD). Individuals must pass a test to receive one of several licenses, the most common being the Series 7—Registered Representative—which enables the individual to sell stocks, bonds, mutual funds, limited partnerships, and a number of other well-known investments. The Series 7 is the license that most financial planners should have. Many also have the higher-level Series 24—Registered Principal license. In all brokerage firms, a Registered Principal license must be held by people in supervisory jobs.

One of the most popular professional designations is Certified Financial Planner (CFP). Anyone with the CFP has completed a two-year study and testing program and has passed six examinations. The program is administered by the College for Financial Planning in Denver, Colorado.

Another designation is Chartered Financial Consultant

(ChFC). A ChFC undergoes a four-year program that includes 10 examinations. This program is administered by the American College in Bryn Mawr, Pennsylvania.

Planners may also be designated individually or through a firm as a Registered Investment Adviser (RIA). This means that the person (or the firm) is registered with the SEC and may give advice about investing in securities.

Many accountants and other professionals offer financial planning services. A qualified accountant should be a state-licensed Certified Public Accountant (CPA). Planners may also have college degrees of various types, including a Master of Science in Financial Services (M.S.F.S.); Bachelor of Laws (LL.B.); Master of Law (LL.M.); or Juris Doctor (J.D.).

The International Association for Financial Planning (IAFP) is the largest membership association of financial planners. It is located at Two Concourse Parkway, Suite 800, Atlanta, GA 30328. Anyone can join by paying an annual fee. The IAFP also sponsors a group called the Registry of Financial Planning Practitioners. To join the registry, an individual must hold a CFP, ChFC, or CPA designation; have a J.D., LL.B., or LL.M. degree or a degree with a major in financial planning; or must complete a financial planning curriculum accredited by the registry. Candidates must also submit an actual financial plan and references from five clients; and before approval and acceptance, they must complete a practical knowledge examination. A final requirement is that the applicant's primary vocation has been as a financial planner for at least three years.

With its specific requirements, the registry provides the most complete screening for a financial planner. A member of the registry is probably the most qualified to offer financial and investing advice. The IAFP will provide referrals to registry members in your area. For another source of local referrals, contact the Investment Management Consultants Association, 10200 E. Girard Avenue, Suite 340C, Denver, CO 80231.

Although it is critically important to check qualifications before retaining a financial adviser, you should first be willing to take responsibility for determining your own investing standards and objectives. Second, you must never trust blindly. Third, you must be willing to apply the standards of investigation and research to selection of an adviser. And finally, to gain confidence, you must accept the idea that any plan of action is *your* plan—defined, developed, and controlled by you and not someone else.

A PERSPECTIVE ON ADVICE

The first assumption most new investors make is that experienced brokers and advisors somehow know the secrets of making money through investing. Thus, they must listen to a more experienced person—a stockbroker, financial planner, or other counselor—to succeed.

In fact, if you adopt the attitude that *you* are responsible for the direction of your financial future, then you will be in charge. That means you determine your own goals, risk standards, and appropriate investments. It does not mean that financial planners are excluded from the process, only that you are in charge.

An adviser can be most useful in suggesting ways to meet your goals.

Example: One individual set the goal of paying off his home mortgage in 10 years. He planned to save money each month to accumulate a lump sum, which would then be paid to the lender. A financial adviser showed him how to achieve the same result by paying an additional amount to the mortgage principal each month.

Another example: You establish a range of acceptable risk and are comparing several possible investments. A financial planner might be able to introduce you to products you have not considered. If any of them fall within your range, they will be worth investigating. A competent financial planner will be able to answer your questions concerning risk attributes of specific investments she suggests to you.

When you work with an adviser, keep in mind that she will be compensated by commission, fee, or both.

1. Commission

An adviser who earns a commission has an unavoidable conflict of interest in representing her services as independent or individually tailored planning.

Example: You visit a financial planner for advice on where to invest $10,000 you recently inherited. The planner presents two or three choices and gives you reasons why they are good investments. (These reasons may include prior performance, diversification, experience of management, or potential for profit.) You must ask yourself, however, why *these* particular investments are being recommended. The truth might be found in the wide range of commission rates the planner will earn based on which investments she suggests to you. Even when a planner is sincerely motivated to help you, it is difficult to remain objective in this situation.

Example: The planner suggests you put your money into a public real estate partnership. The program will remain in effect for as long as 10 years, and, in fact, you will have difficulty getting your money out sooner. A comparable real estate investment trust may yield better and is also completely liquid (you can trade in your shares on the public stock exchanges) but this program is not recommended to you. Why not?

The answer is in the commission rate. A partnership might offer 12 percent to the planner, while the trust pays only 8 percent. Her compensation is thus 50 percent higher for selling units in the partnership.

2. Fee Planning

Today, many planners no longer accept traditional commission-based compensation. They see it as too closely associated with pure sales (and planners would like to be perceived as more dignified professionals) and recognize the conflict of interest it creates.

Some planners offer a pure consultation service. Rates vary:

Some charge $50 or less for an hour's consultation; others charge $200 for the same thing. And you have no way of knowing in advance how valuable that consultation will be.

3. Commissions and Fees

Even the planners who claim to charge only a fee will often earn commissions on top of the fee. Not only is this a form of double compensation, it also means that the same conflict of interest is present.

The problem is caused, in part, by the regulatory environment of the securities industry. A licensed salesperson *must* be paid a commission for all business placed for clients. So even the planner who wants to accept fees alone must, by law, be compensated twice.

The only way around this problem is for the planner to refer you to someone else, who will earn a commission for business placed. But most planners resist this idea. It is not only inconvenient; if they are licensed to place business, they reason, why should they send their clients elsewhere?

Still, many planners attempt to create the appearance of being completely free of conflicts—and yet they are not. Some examples:

1. A planner tells his clients that he receives absolutely no compensation beyond the fee he charges for consultation. This may be strictly true in a legal sense, but untrue in reality. He has set up a corporation to which he assigns the commissions his broker-dealer pays him. Thus, he has taken the commission from his private pocket and put it in his corporate pocket. Since he is the sole stockholder in that corporation, what's the difference?
2. A planner advertises that she collects a fee and nothing else. For placement of business, she refers clients to another licensed representative down the hall. Unknown to the client, though, is that when the commission is calculated, the second representative will split the commission with the planner, often paying her back the largest share. Splitting fees

between registered representatives is perfectly legal from the broker-dealer's point of view; it simply means that both individuals worked on the case.
3. Two planners, each generating approximately the same level of volume, tell clients that they work for fees alone. They refer clients to each other for actual placement. On the bottom line, they both come out with double compensation.

How do you deal with this problem? Because commission payments are still universal in securities sales, you should be aware that whenever you write a check for an investment made through a planner, a commission is going to be paid to someone (unless you invest strictly in no-load products). The solution is to ask a planner how she is compensated before agreeing to pay for services. If a fee is charged, you should know in advance how it is computed (flat fee, hourly rate, or percentage of your net worth, for example) and when payments are to be made. Also, an ethical planner will tell you if she receives a commission on any investments you make.

Whether that information is volunteered or not, you should plan to ask about compensation. And when the planner recommends an investment, ask what the percentage of commission will be. Remember that *you* pay the commission directly. For example, if the rate is 12 percent, that means that only 88 cents of every dollar you invest goes to work for you. The remainder goes directly to the planner.

Example: A planner discusses three different investments with you. They seem comparable in all respects, but the planner suggests one over the other two. You ask the commission rate she will receive on each one and discover that the rate is higher for the one being recommended.

The decision on where to invest your money remains yours. Keeping this perspective, you can see the outside adviser as useful in two ways: first, as yet another source for information and advice and as a check on the validity of your ideas; and second, as the conduit for placing your investment.

THE DISCOUNT BROKER

When investing in the stock market, you can avoid the problem of commissions and the obvious conflicts of interest by using a discount broker.

To many people, this arrangement makes good sense. Instead of paying full commissions to a broker—especially when you do your own research and investigation—you pay a discounter for only one service: placing your trades. A discount broker charges a much smaller transaction fee for this service —savings can be as great as 70 percent (sometimes more for large trades). And if you are an active trader, using a discount broker makes a lot of sense. The cost of trading commissions paid to a full-commission broker becomes a significant factor in the total cost of investing.

Discounting is a relatively new concept. It has been allowed only since the mid-1970s, when the SEC removed regulatory controls over the fees charged by brokerage firms. When that occurred, most firms raised their fees substantially. A few went into the discount business.

With discounters as an alternative, you might wonder if you really get your money's worth from a full-commission firm. That is a question you must answer for yourself. If you depend on the advice of a stockbroker, you will not benefit from working with discounters. They provide no advice and do not solicit business. Also, to many investors, the idea of leaving the apparent security of a brokerage relationship is too much of a threat. And a talented, capable broker whose timing and advice have always been good is someone worth keeping on your team.

Unfortunately, the majority of individual investors have not had brokers like that. Like financial planners, brokers are paid by commission. Their motive is to sell, and the greater the volume of transactions, the greater their income.

Contact discount brokerage firms in your area and compare services. To pick one best suited to you, keep these points in mind:

1. A local firm is more convenient and easier to work with because you can visit the office to submit paperwork, ask questions, and deal with other account business.

2. A firm that offers a wide range of investments is good. The larger discounters are set up for stocks, bonds, mutual funds, and option trading. Some also allow you to buy units of public partnerships.
3. The commission rate varies from one firm to another. Look beyond the fee itself and evaluate the range of services. Some firms offer online trading through home computers, networking and quotation services, toll-free phone lines, and free educational literature.

DEFINING SAFETY

Commission-based brokerage firms and financial planners must justify their commissions by offering service—or the appearance of service. A discount brokerage firm offers one thing: transaction placement. If that's all you need, that's all you should be paying for. In fact, however, the investing public has been demanding an increasing level of service from brokers and planners for many years. Whether a firm or an individual can meet that demand is something you'll have to determine for yourself.

Recognizing the public demand for service, planners try to create the appearance of objectivity. They claim to tailor a plan to suit your individual needs and objectives. The truth is that most planners are insurance and securities salespeople, and they do not really understand the concept of defining safety or the idea of working from specific objectives.

Planners promote a product by describing it in terms of investment objectives. For example, one will tell you that the objective of a public syndication is "income, protection against inflation, tax-free income, and appreciation of capital." In reality, those are not objectives. They are only attributes of a program that should be used to determine whether or not it suits your standards for acceptable risk.

An objective relates to your purpose in making an investment and the kind of investor you are. A speculator is interested only in speculative, short-term income; a moderate seeks diversification between income and growth; and a conservative wants insured accounts and a very low chance for future losses.

Yield and growth will be determined by the type of investment you make: The higher the risk, the greater the chance for profit, or for loss. Nevertheless, the objective must always rule.

Example: If your objective is to save money for a down payment on a house you want to buy within five years, you would be ill-advised to put your money into an illiquid investment that will stay in effect for 10 years or more. Similarly, if you have a limited fund and want to preserve it, buying highly speculative stocks would be reckless beyond your standards.

DEVELOPING A PLAN

The financial planning community places great emphasis on the need for professional help in devising a plan. But for a plan to be your own, you must be the captain of the ship. You cannot delegate the responsibility for your financial future to someone who is thinking about the short term, that is, earning commissions this month and this year.

A plan should be straightforward and simple. You have an objective or series of objectives. These are broken down into a series of goals. It should be mentioned here that "goals" and "objectives" often mean one and the same thing. The terms are thrown around by financial planners, often without definition. For our purposes, an objective is the overall purpose for investing, and a goal is the means by which you will achieve a phase of that objective.

Example: You are planning ahead to buy your first house. You will need to save enough money for a down payment. The objective is to purchase a house. The goals can include:

1. Devising a family budget that will enable you to save the same amount each month.
2. Finding investments that suit your safety and risk standards.
3. Creating a realistic deadline for achieving the objective.

Goals must have deadlines or they will never be realized. Develop your plan—assuming you already understand your long-term objective—on the foundation of a series of specific goals and their deadlines for completion.

A plan must also change. For example, your objective today is to buy a house, and you plan for that through a series of goals and deadlines. But once you have your house, a new objective must replace the old one. As your family grows, as your career develops, and as you and your spouse begin to age, new priorities emerge:

- ☐ Retirement
- ☐ Insurance (life, health, home, etc.)
- ☐ College education
- ☐ The *next* house
- ☐ Career alternatives

With a new objective, your original plan becomes obsolete; so as you change your lifestyle and priorities, you will also need to reevaluate your investment plan.

An interesting thing happens when you change. Everything about your plan must change as well, including your safety and risk standards. What once were absolute risk limits may now expand or contract as your annual income changes, as you accumulate net worth, and as you grow older.

DEVELOPING YOUR OWN PLAN

A plan is a fairly simple idea that exists in your own mind and results from definition, research, and knowledge. What you put down on paper is only a guideline you create for yourself; there is no universally dictated format for a plan.

To some people, a plan does not exist until there is a computer-generated, bound document complete with projections, calculations, worksheets, assumptions, and recommendations. In truth, these are not planning features at all. A plan should be tangible within your mind, and that does not require an impressive appearance but rather a concrete idea of what you want and how to get it.

The starting point is always your objective. Once you understand *why* you need a plan, developing it is a simple process. Follow these steps:

1. Identify goals

Make up a list of action steps you must take in order to achieve your objective. Don't try to achieve the entire objective in one step; break it down into phases. And set realistic deadlines for yourself.

2. Define risk limits

Even if you have already decided how much risk is proper for you, take another look. Once you have identified a tangible objective, you might discover that your preconceived ideas of risk have changed.

In some cases, how important an objective is alters the degree of risk you're willing to take. So a reevaluation is always in order during this phase of the planning process.

3. Prepare the plan

Write down the steps you intend to take. Put down on paper your major objective and then write out the goals you have established to reach it. Also write down your deadline for each goal.

Prepare a series of simple scheduling charts, and then track your own progress. The real planning goes on in your mind, but tracking your progress is important to achieving success. You make your goals tangible when you have them down on paper and when you see gradual progress.

4. Pick investments

Once you know where you are going and what you mean to achieve, you must next decide where to put your money. The answer depends not only on the objective but on your definition of risk and safety—and these are not constants.

You will also need to investigate and research in depth to find the best possible investment—within the scope of *your* definitions. A professional planner can make suggestions or recommend products, but be sure you evaluate these suggestions in terms of what you want.

5. *Take action*
There is a time to plan, and there is a time to act. Once you are satisfied with your preliminary defining and research, make a decision and take action.

6. *Remain flexible*
The last phase of the planning process is one of the most important. To many people, once an investment decision has been made, the story is over. In fact, the decision should be the beginning, the place where real planning starts.

What you consider an important goal today will seem insignificant in a year, five years, or ten years. Today's risk limits

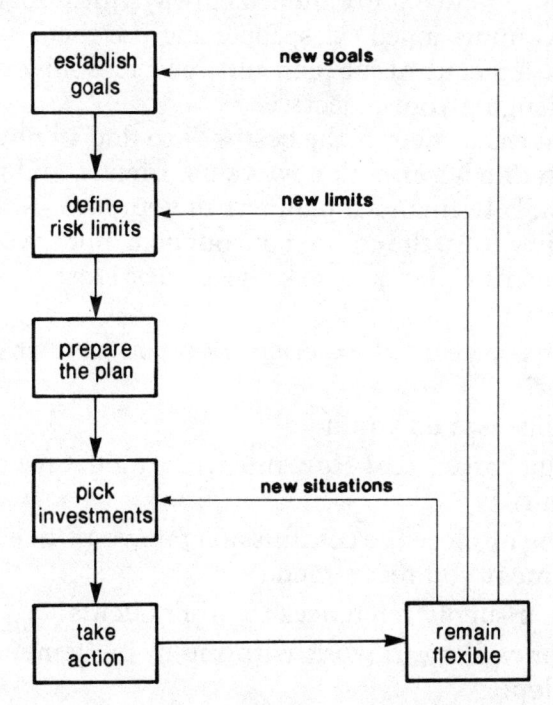

Figure 10-1. Developing the Plan

will be affected by changes in your family status and income, and your own maturity. And few investments are permanent; economic situations change, and new opportunities constantly come up.

You must be willing to continually reevaluate your entire plan. Be willing to establish new goals and risk limits, and to change investments on the basis of changing situations.

The process of developing your own plan is shown in Figure 10-1.

WORKING WITH PLANNERS

A simple plan, developed individually, is the most effective means for achieving your financial goals. Without a plan, you have no specific purpose in making investments. With one, you have a clear focus on your future.

Entering a new environment is always intimidating; so do work with commissioned salespeople and use them as resources —as long as you control the plan and don't let someone else talk you into changing your objective.

The referral system is the best way to find a knowledgeable and competent adviser. Ask coworkers, friends, and professionals for referrals to financial planners in your area. And use their services only within the context of your plan, under your control.

In comparing planners, ask these questions:

1. How many years of experience do you have as a financial planner?
2. What licenses do you hold?
3. Do you charge a fee? How much? Is it a flat fee or so much per hour?
4. Will you disclose the commission rate you will earn on each investment you recommend?
5. Will you supply references to other clients?
6. Are you willing to work with me in implementing a plan I develop?

7. Are you a specialist? If so, what is your emphasis and background? (Some planners emphasize insurance, public partnerships, or mutual funds, for example.)

Keep planning advice in perspective, and seek it only after you develop your plan. Listen carefully. When salespeople advise you to change part of your plan, what are they really saying? Do their arguments make sense to you within the context of your objectives?

Many very successful, confident, and ethical people make a living as financial planners. If you look, you will recognize them without trouble. They are the ones who, when you approach them with your plan, promptly and gladly work with you and respect your diligence. They will not feel threatened by the approach you take or by your insistence on being in control of your own future.

11

HOW TO TRACK YOUR INVESTMENTS

If you do something once, people will call it an accident. If you do it twice, they call it a coincidence. But do it a third time and you've just proven a natural law.

Grace Murray Hopper

Misconceptions about the market lead many investors astray. There is a cult of belief that, somehow, there is a formula for consistently beating the system and creating wealth. If there were such a system, the market itself would not exist as it is. We could all become wealthy, and wealth would no longer be meaningful.

This logic is forgotten by those who employ wishful thinking rather than intelligence as an approach to investing. There is a progression of experience that every investor goes through, beginning with initial learning experiences and then reaching the point where decisions must be made—not just about where to invest but about what philosophy to follow.

The progression follows these steps:

1. The search for advice

Most investors start out looking for guidance from someone. Typically, when the beginner walks into a brokerage firm he is referred to the "broker of the day." Thus, ironically, the inexperienced investor has placed his trust in the most inexperienced broker available.

The search may begin in other ways. Many brokerage firms start their new representatives out by having them telephone people with "opportunities" in the market.

2. *The first experience*
When an individual starts out investing in the usual, passive way, his first experience is usually a negative one—perhaps he puts a limited amount of money into securities that lose money. But, more to the point, the method of selection, because it is passive and ill-conceived, does not match the investor's personal investing standards. In fact, at this point, most novice investors have not even begun to develop their standards.

3. *Reevaluation*
After the initial experience, the new investor reevaluates, perhaps concluding that the wrong broker was used, that the timing was wrong, or that sinister economic forces subverted an otherwise sound effort.

Regardless of the reason an investment does not work out, the fact remains that the approach was wrong. If the investor is to learn from this initial experience, he must begin again at the right place: defining criteria.

4. *A new approach*
This is the critical phase. If the investor truly learns from the first, bad investment, he will be a little poorer but much wiser. Unfortunately, many people draw the wrong conclusion from this experience. They either avoid investing altogether (assuming they cannot win) or they begin searching for a magic formula for market success.

Those who recognize the flaw in their first attempt discover that taking responsibility for their own decisions is the real answer. For this group, the first experience in the market—even though money was lost—ends up being the best investment they could have made. The value of experience cannot be matched by early profits.

DEFINING YOUR STANDARDS

It is easy to say, "Define your risk standard," but much more difficult to arrive at a definition. For many investors, the process takes years of misguided experimentation and testing. This is both costly and discouraging.

The process of deciding how to approach the market is elusive for those who don't see the need for research, definition, and analysis. Many people never arrive at a clear definition, nor do they ever learn that no secret formula exists. And some attach their hopes to a singular theory, following it blindly and accepting loss after loss. These investors never truly learn from experience.

The challenge all investors face is arriving at a conclusive, definite series of criteria that are based on personal investing standards, types of investments, ultimate goals, and the degree of knowledge accumulated. You must be prepared to decide how much weight to give to various forms of analysis, how to collect and compare data, and how to interpret what you learn by taking action.

You will learn a great deal by listening to other investors. You will hear statements like, "I bought into XYZ company last week, and it's already gone up four points," or "My broker recommended this new issue. This company's stock is going to go through the roof." What you *won't* hear anyone saying is, "I decided to buy the stock because the fundamentals were strong," or "All the indicators were clear. It was the right time to buy." The startling reality is that, although much is written about forms of analysis and approaches to the market, few people have clearly defined their own approach. In general, investors make their decisions inconsistently and intuitively.

If you subscribe to a particular theory of investing, you must follow the rules of that theory. We learn nothing by adopting a point of view, only to break the rules that go with it. Given that attaining success as an investor is no easy task, and that no one method guarantees it, we need to discipline ourselves by first setting, and then following, rules.

If there is any secret to investing, it is working from a clear definition, that is, defining all potential investments in terms of how they fit your model of a good risk. It doesn't matter that you depend on fundamental or technical analysis, or both, or whether you read annual reports and financial statements. What does matter is that you develop your own approach and then follow it. This is the single rule that every investor should follow, and the one basic and essential point that most investors miss.

Once you understand the meaning and value of various types of information, you must choose your own series of criteria. For example, you might take the following approach:

1. Isolate specific industries and analyze the fundamentally strongest companies in those industries.
2. Track price, P/E ratio, dividend yield, volatility, and volume to identify stocks that fit your established standards for safety, yield, and price stability.
3. Track specific fundamental signs to identify companies that have a clear track record of growth and financial strength.

This process will help you identify companies that match your standard for investing. Prepare a stock selection worksheet like the one shown in Figure 11-1.

The first section of the worksheet tracks the information from the daily stock listings in your financial newspaper. Follow your target stocks for several weeks, writing in the information listed at the end of each week. Collect data from five days of trading and prepare a weekly summary. This example gives weight to the details listed, but it is assumed that you will research each company you track using other details as well.

This worksheet also assumes that you know how to interpret the various forms of information. If you can draw conclusions from volume trends, for example, that certainly helps you select or eliminate a stock. One standard you set for yourself might be that you will buy stocks that are not too close in price to the 52-week high and low range, and you might further decide that volatility should be below 20 percent. (Volatility is computed by subtracting the 52-week low from the high and dividing the result by the low.) You could also look for stocks with consistency in volume levels.

stock selection worksheet

company _____ date _____

DATE	PRICE	P/E RATIO	DIVIDEND YIELD	52-WEEK HIGH	52-WEEK LOW	VOLATILITY	VOLUME

	YEAR ___	YEAR ___	YEAR ___	YEAR ___
Dividends per share				
Earnings per share				
Book value per share				
Average P/E ratio				
Annual sales				
Operating margin				
Net profits				

Figure 11-1. Stock Selection Worksheet

The problem of finding the significance in information is one that every investor must solve individually. For example, what if the level of volume for the stock you're tracking increases suddenly? What does that mean? Some investors will assume it is a signal of renewed interest in the stock; others will see it as a danger signal. It all depends on who is buying and why, or who is selling and why. The solution, of course, goes back to your ability to understand the meaning of a changing trend and how it will affect future market price.

The second box on the worksheet lists four years of fundamentals. Remember that the fundamental signals must be viewed as part of a trend. Most investors will agree that a consistent pattern of growth is more desirable than a pattern of widely varying ups and downs. For example, the annual sales, operating margin, and net profits should show steady growth or, at least, consistent levels each year. This is only one point of view, of course, and you must decide for yourself what is significant and what should be tracked. Ultimately, you must make your investment decision on the basis of what you believe to be valid.

TRACKING YOUR HOLDINGS

How can you determine if your system is working? It is not enough to decide on a formula to judge your own success; you must also be able to monitor progress and make adjustments as you discover flaws.

Also, your point of view will change as you gain investing experience. Be willing to change your strategies; to abandon yesterday's ideas; and to accept the fact that your acceptable risk levels will change with time, economic status, and experience. No one philosophy or approach to the market should remain unchanged. Successful investors must be willing to learn, to change, and to grow.

Use a form to track your investment—not only to determine when your profit target has been reached, but also to test and judge the criteria you are using. A sample form is shown in Figure 11-2.

Figure 11-2 is a form for a single investment, with lines for the purchase price and date and the target price. A line is also included for the bail-out price.

Example: You buy 300 shares of stock at $28 per share. Your target goal is $38 per share; however, you will also sell if the stock's value falls to $24 per share.

Upon sale, the date and price are entered, and the profit or loss is computed. Throughout the holding period, price movement is tracked on the chart at the bottom of the form. The share price and dates should be written in at the end of each week.

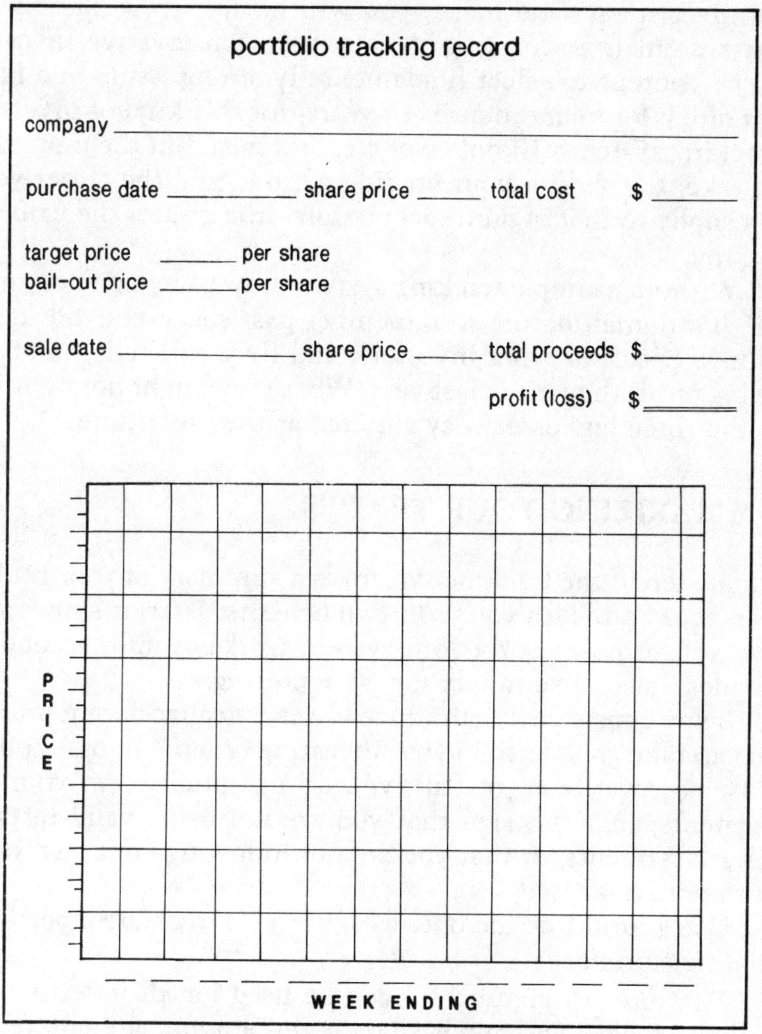

portfolio tracking record

company _____

purchase date _____ share price _____ total cost $ _____

target price _____ per share
bail-out price _____ per share

sale date _____ share price _____ total proceeds $_____

profit (loss) $_____

PRICE / WEEK ENDING

Figure 11-2. Portfolio Tracking Record

If you give any weight to patterns in charts, you will find this analysis a useful one. Some theorists believe that individual stocks set a recurring price pattern. If you believe this, you will be able to use the chart to (1) anticipate buy and sell signals, and (2) recognize pattern trends as they recur.

By tracking your holdings consistently and comparing various investments you make, you will be able to see how well your system is performing. A relatively conservative investor will be content to select fundamentally strong issues and hold their stock for many months or years; for this kind of investor, a tracking system will not be of great interest. But the more risk you take, the shorter your holding periods, and the closer your philosophy to that of pure speculation—the greater the value of tracking.

Without a simple tracking system, how can you judge yourself? It's human nature to remember past successes and forget failures. Speak to other investors, and they will tell you about the big profit they made last year. What they might not mention are the three big losses they suffered at the same time.

SUMMARIZING YOUR TRADES

A final step in the tracking system is a summary of your trades. This record provides you with two benefits: First, it shows you how well or how poorly your system works overall; second, it provides a useful summary for tax reporting.

If you consistently minimize losses or realize decent profits, you can take great faith in your investing criteria. If losses offset gains, however, and, overall, you do not profit from your investments, that is a sign that you are not using valid tests to pick investments, or that you are not following your own rules consistently.

Use a form like the one in Figure 11-3 to create a portfolio tracking summary.

The form in Figure 11-3 can be used for all investments, not just stocks. The purchase date and amount are entered at the time of purchase, as shown in this example:

Description	Purchase date	Amount
300 shares, XYZ	3/20/89	$1,932.15

When each investment is sold, the sale date and amount are entered. The sale price less the purchase price is the amount of profit. If there is a loss, the total is enclosed in brackets.

trading summary

YEAR ______

DESCRIPTION	PURCHASE DATE	AMOUNT	SALE DATE	AMOUNT	PROFIT (LOSS)	YIELD	ANNUAL YIELD
TOTAL							

Figure 11-3. Trading Summary

The yield is computed on the basis of your purchase price. For example, you sell your 300 shares of XYZ on October 20, 1989 and receive a total of $2,314.45. That is a profit of $382.30:

$$\begin{array}{ll} \text{Sale price} & \$2,314.45 \\ \text{Less: Purchase price} & 1,932.15 \\ \text{Profit} & \$382.30 \end{array}$$

The yield is 19.8 percent:

$$\frac{382.30}{1,932.15} = 19.8\%$$

Next, the yield should be annualized, or expressed on the basis of 12 months' return, so that you can compare your profits and losses on the same basis. If you earn a 19.8 percent profit over seven months, as in the example above, the annualized yield will be different than if you earn the same profit over three years.

To annualize your return, divide the yield by the number of months held, and then multiply the sum by 12:

$$\frac{19.7}{7} \times 12 = 33.8\%$$

To see how differently an annual yield compares, calculate what the yield would be if you held this stock for 36 months:

$$\frac{19.7}{36} \times 12 = 6.6\%$$

EVALUATING YOUR OWN STANDARDS

Defining and applying standards is a major accomplishment for any investor. If you are able to do this, and discipline yourself to follow a set of rules, your chances for success are much better than those for the average investor. But once you have achieved this, you must also be prepared to change—to reevaluate your entire approach—when it becomes necessary.

Review your past investments—especially those in which you lost money—against the criteria you used. In order for this analysis to be valid, it is crucial that you applied the same series of tests to the companies and researched them thoroughly. If you keep records of what you test and analyze and how your investments fare, you will be able to judge the effectiveness of your standards.

Example: One investor limited his investments to three leading industries. He also tested earnings per share, dividends per share and net profits over the previous four years. Finally, he computed volatility at the time of purchase.

He discovered that when the market fell (according to changes in the Dow Jones Industrial Averages), stocks with lower volatility tended to lose less, and when the market rose, higher-volatility stocks tended to gain more.

This information was useful in evaluating the tests conducted before investing. Based on the degree of risk this investor was willing to take, the question of volatility became critical. Those investments that realized a loss were usually in stocks with higher volatility rates. The conclusion: Choosing stocks with lower volatility might limit potential gains when the market rises, but high-volatility stocks represent greater risks when the market falls.

The example—using volatility as a crucial factor—is a generalization, but it shows how one bit of information can be invaluable. When applied in a broad sense to determine what is good or safe, the information is meaningless, but when used to test an investment's viability *against a well-defined standard for risk*, it becomes significant.

Investment selection must be based on a number of different tests, each given appropriate weight in your final decision. It is a mistake, for example, to label yourself a conservative and buy only those stocks with low volatility, and it is equally unwise to apply criteria that, according to past experience, do not affect the performance of your investments.

Example: One investor bought only stocks whose book value was equal to or greater than market price, until he discovered that those stocks tended to perform poorly. His original belief was that book value substantially affected the actual market price. Experience taught him, however, that the trend in book value was one of many factors to consider, but by itself meant very little in determining future potential.

No one can claim with any valid proof that one or even a series of criteria will guarantee any degree of success. The combination of numerous technical and fundamental indicators will help improve your knowledge, but it can also cloud your judgment. If you depend on misconceptions, such as the common belief about the real meaning of the P/E ratio, then you cannot expect much profit. Any indicator that relates purely to the past cannot, by nature, be counted on to predict the future.

The answer is to develop a program that includes a series of tests, with the central idea that knowledge and research lead to profits. The combination of facts you use should be designed to: (1) identify industries and stocks or other forms of investment that represent viable candidates; (2) eliminate inappropriate investments in order to narrow your field of choice; and (3) apply your well-defined risk and safety standards to every investment being considered, within the context of your personal objectives.

If there is a magic formula for successful investing, it is the consistent application of an intelligent approach. If you are willing to compare choices, define and redefine your comfort zones, and evaluate constantly, you will be in the best position to make your own decisions. As a successful investor, you will understand and apply the sensible rules you establish for yourself. And you will discover the satisfaction that comes from taking charge of your own financial future.

GLOSSARY

accumulation area in technical analysis, a price range near the support level, or the lowest general range in which investors are willing to purchase shares.

acid test ratio alternate name for the **quick assets ratio**.

active market a single stock, group of stocks, or the market as a whole, when trading volume is heavy.

adjusted basis the amount paid for an investment after adding brokerage commissions.

advance–decline index an index that compares daily issues that rose or fell, tracking the net advances or declines to spot a trend or anticipate future market movement.

American Stock Exchange 86 Trinity Place, New York, NY 10006. Called the New York Curb Exchange until 1921, the Amex is the second-largest stock exchange in the United States.

annual report 1) an operational summary issued by corporations that includes audited financial statements, comments on markets for the preceding year, estimates of the future, and a message from the chief executive officer;

2) form 10-K, a detailed financial summary that every publicly registered corporation must file each year with the Securities and Exchange Commission.

asked price the lowest price at which the owner of a security is willing to sell; also called the **quotation.** In comparison, a bid is the highest price a potential buyer is willing to pay.

assets properties owned by a corporation.

at risk limitations the ceiling allowed on deduction of losses for investors in limited partnerships and other passive investments.

at the close the price of a security at the close of the market each day; or an order to buy or sell a security at the closing price.

at the market the most common form of order to buy or sell securities at the prevailing market price.

at the opening the price of securities at the time the market opens; or an order to execute a transaction at the opening price or as soon thereafter.

auction marketplace a market, such as the stock exchange, in which buyers and sellers negotiate prices based on supply and demand.

automatic reinvestment an option available to investors in mutual funds, under which all income from dividends, interest, and capital gains distributions is applied toward the purchase of additional shares.

average down an investing technique in which additional shares of a security are purchased after the price has fallen. The result is to create an average basis in the investment between current market value and the higher original purchase price.

average up an investing technique in which additional shares of a security are purchased after the price has risen. The result is to create an average basis in the investment between current market value and the lower original purchase price.

averages the measurement of market value, derived from the collective analysis of a group of stocks. The best-known are the Dow Jones Industrial Averages (DJIA) and the Standard & Poor's 500 Composite index.

balance sheet a financial statement that shows the value of total assets, liabilities, and net worth as of a specified date. Total assets are equal to the sum of liabilities plus net worth.

balanced company a type of mutual fund that diversifies its total portfolio between bonds and common and preferred stocks. The purpose is to achieve a balance between growth and income.

Barron's Confidence Index an index of stock market sentiment, based on trends in low-grade bond yields. This index is based on the theory that as the yield falls, sentiment favors the stock market.

basis the total cost of acquiring a holding in a security, consisting of the purchase price and commissions charged.

bear an individual who believes the stock market will fall in the immediate future, or a market in which the signs point to falling prices.

beta a measurement of relative volatility in stocks, compared to the market as a whole. A beta factor of 1 is assigned to stocks that move in the same degree as the market. Extremely volatile stocks may be assigned a beta as high as 2.

bid price the highest price a potential buyer of a security is willing to pay. In comparison, an offer is the lowest price at which an owner is willing to sell.

big board the New York Stock Exchange and the trading activity that occurs there.

block a transaction in one stock of 10,000 shares or more; a size of trade made by institutional investors.

blue chip the stock of a company with a long and established history of performance; often applied to stock of one of the companies included in the Dow Jones Industrial Averages (DJIA).

boiler room an operation that solicits business on the telephone, employing high-pressure tactics for questionable and speculative products.

bond a debt obligation issued by a government, government agency, or corporation, in denominations of $1000 or more and payable in five years or more. The bond is secured by revenues, future income, full faith and credit of the issuer, mortgages, or other assets.

bond fund a mutual fund that invests in a number of diversified corporate and government bonds. Some bond funds specialize in tax-exempt bonds.

book value the tangible equity of a corporation, represented by total assets (without intangible assets) minus all liabilities.

book value per share the book value of a corporation divided by the number of shares of outstanding common stock.

breadth of the market a measure of changes in the advance–decline index, computed by subtracting declining issues from advancing issues, and dividing the sum by total issues traded. The resulting percentage is that day's breadth index.

breakaway gap a term used by chartists to describe a gap between price ranges from one day to the next. A stock's opening price is higher or lower than the closing price of the previous day, creating the price range gap, or a breakaway from the previously established trading range.

breakout a term used by technicians to describe price movement in a stock. It occurs when the trading range breaks through a resistance level (upward price movement) or support level (downward movement).

breakpoint a purchase amount above which the rate of mutual fund sales load is reduced.

bull an individual who believes the stock market will rise in the immediate future, or a market in which the signs point to rising prices.

buying climax a sudden and unexpected increase in the trading range and price of a security.

capital the total equity of a corporation, made up of (1) the combined value of issued stock, (2) additional issues of stock, and (3) retained earnings from prior years; and reduced by losses and dividends declared and paid.

capital appreciation an investment purpose stated by management of a mutual fund or by individual investors, meaning that investments will be made with the aim of growth in the value of capital.

capital gain or loss a net profit or loss from the purchase and sale of securities and other assets. When proceeds upon sale exceed the net basis price, a capital gain results; when the sale proceeds are less than the purchase amount, a capital loss results.

capital market a broad description of markets that provide intermediate and long-term capital for business funding, including U.S. government securities, federal agency debts, corporate bonds, state and local government bonds, mortgages, and capital stock. In comparison, short-term funding is broadly described as the money market.

capital preservation an investment purpose stated by management of a mutual fund or savings institution, or by an individual, meaning that investments will be made with the aim of protecting or insuring the safety of capital.

capital stock the total invested equity of a corporation, combining the value of common and preferred stock.

capitalization the total funding of a corporation, made up of both equity (common and preferred stock) and debt capital (bonds, debentures, and loans).

cash flow the availability of cash in a corporation, an important measurement of management's ability to time income and payments. The consistent generation of cash is critical to successful operations; it is required to pay current debts and to invest in inventories, expansion, and capital assets.

cash-on-cash return a simplified method for computing the return on an investment. The amount of cash received (in the form of dividends, interest, or capital gains distributions) is divided by the original investment, without regard for the timing of those payments.

Certified Financial Planner (CFP) the most widely acknowledged degree in the planning industry, granted to individuals who have successfully passed a series of examinations administered by the College for Financial Planning.

chartist a technician who estimates future price movement based on the study of trading patterns in a stock or in the market as a whole. Chartists believe that certain patterns foretell future price movements, and that stocks establish trading patterns that are repeated.

churning the unethical practice on the part of a broker of creating transactions in a client's account to generate commissions rather than to benefit the client.

close 1) the last 30 seconds of the trading day on a stock exchange;

2) the price at which a stock closes for the day.

closed-end fund a mutual fund that issues only a fixed number of shares. Once it is fully issued, individuals may buy into the fund only by purchasing shares from other investors. In comparison, the more common open-end fund will issue as many shares as there are interested investors.

closed position a canceled position. If the investor was "long," meaning securities were previously purchased, the position is closed by selling. If the investor was "short," meaning securities were previously sold, the position is closed by buying.

closing price the price of stock at the end of the trading day.

collateral assets pledged as a promise to pay a debt. For example, when investors trade on margin, a percentage of the total risk must be left on deposit with the broker as collateral.

commingled funds accounts in which the funds of different clients are combined, a practice that brokerage firms are prohibited from employing.

commission the amount of money paid to a stockbroker, account executive, financial planner, adviser, consultant, or other salesperson. It is computed as a percentage of the amount the client invests.

commodity a consumer good for which future delivery is ensured through a futures contract. A future price is agreed upon by both buyer and seller, and the actual value of a commodity future contract then varies on the basis of actual supply and demand.

common stock the equity in a corporation, made up of a number of shares held by investors. In the event of liquidation, the common stockholder is paid last, after bondholders, creditors, and preferred stockholders.

composite index an index combining the values of a number of securities or other indexes.

conflict of interest a situation in which an individual or entity could benefit directly by making decisions affecting investors. In a limited partnership, the question of conflict of interest should be applied in an evaluation of the general partners.

convertible security bonds or preferred stock that can be exchanged for shares of common stock.

corporation a business entity that is commonly owned, with each owner holding a number of shares.

cost of goods sold costs incurred in direct relationship to production of revenues. When subtracted from revenues, the result is a company's gross profit.

cum dividend without the dividend; reference to ownership in stock after the dividend payment date.

current assets assets that are cash or convertible to cash within one year (including accounts receivable, inventories, and marketable securities).

current liabilities all debts that are due and payable within one year, including accounts and taxes payable, accrued liabilities, and the next 12 months' payments due on notes.

current ratio a ratio that evaluates the trend in available working capital. It is derived by dividing current assets by current liabilities.

debt/equity ratio a ratio that examines the relationship between long-term debt and shareholders' equity. The purpose is to determine the portion of total capitalization represented by debt financing.

debt security any investment in which capital is lent to the issuer or institution, subject to redemption on demand or by a future contractual date, that will also earn interest during the holding period.

delivery the transfer of securities from the seller to the buyer.

direct participation program a limited partnership arrangement, in which a large number of investors (limited partners) pool their funds under the management of general partners.

discount 1) the market price of a bond that is available for less than its face value;
2) a reduction in the load fee upon purchase of mutual fund shares, offered when a large amount of capital is invested.

discount broker a brokerage firm that charges a transaction fee that is less than the commissions charged by other brokerage firms. The firm offers no advice or recommendations, only the service of executing buy and sell orders.

discount yield a method for computing yield when securities, such as U.S. Treasury bills, are purchased at discount. Annual discount is divided by the face value to arrive at the annual yield.

discounted cash flow a method for computing yield on an investment that includes the differences in time value of money and tax benefits.

discretionary account a brokerage account in which the client has granted the broker the right to control investment decisions.

distribution area in technical analysis, a price range near the resistance level, or the highest general range in which investors are willing to buy shares.

diversification a principle in investing stating that capital should not be placed in any one security, or in a range of securities that are likely to move in the same direction at the same time.

dividend a distribution of income from a corporation to its shareholders, either in cash or additional stock (a stock dividend).

dividend yield the percentage earned by stockholders, computed by dividing the dividend rate per share by the current market price.

double bottom a charting pattern in which the price range tests a support level twice. Chartists believe this is a sign of strong support, which foretells a rise in trading range.

double top a charting pattern in which the price range tests a resistance level twice. Chartists interpret this as a sign of strong resistance, which foretells a decline in trading range.

Dow Jones Composite Averages an index combining all 65 stocks in the Industrial, Transportation, and Utility Averages.

Dow Jones Industrial Averages (DJIA) the most popular index of the stock market, consisting of price-weighted movements in the stock of 30 major corporations, also called blue chips.

Dow Jones Transportation Averages an index of the price movements in the stock of 20 rail, airline, trucking, and other transportation companies.

Dow Jones Utility Averages an index of the price movements in the stock of 15 public utility companies.

Dow Theory a theory of technical analysis, stating that market trends follow the averages of stock prices.

earnings per share the net income for a specified period of time (usually one full year), divided by the total number of outstanding shares of common stock.

8-K report a report a publicly held corporation must file with the SEC to disclose material changes in ownership, financial strength, acquisitions, and management.

equity security any form of investment in which funds are applied towards the purchase of equity. The best-known example is common stock. In comparison, a debt security (such as a bond) involves lending money to the issuer.

exchange business all transactions taking place over an exchange, including stocks, bonds, commodities, and options.

exdividend date the date from which no dividends are accrued, which follows the record date. Orders placed four business days prior to the record date will not be entitled to the dividend, since transfer of ownership occurs on the fifth day.

face value the par value of a bond; the amount that will be paid upon maturity.

family of funds mutual fund organizations that offer several different funds to investors and allow switching of holdings between funds.

Federal Deposit Insurance Corporation (FDIC) an organization that provides insurance to depositors in member banks, to a stated maximum per account.

Federal Savings and Loan Insurance Corporation (FSLIC) an organization that provides insurance to depositors in member savings and loan associations, to a stated maximum per account.

financial futures futures contracts on interest rates, based on treasury securities, mortgage pools, and certificates of deposit.

financial plan a plan for the control of future finances, designed to plot the achievement of specific investment objectives within a well-defined range of risk.

financial statement a report on financial condition or results of operation. The balance sheet summarizes the balances of asset, liability, and net worth accounts as of a specified date. An income statement reports the sales, costs, expenses, and profits or losses for a stated period of time, normally one full year.

fixed assets alternative name for **long-term assets**.

flat market a market in a security or group of securities when trading volume is low.

Form 10-K a detailed financial report that registered corporations must file every year with the Securities and Exchange Commission.

Form 10-Q a financial report that registered corporations file each quarter with the Securities and Exchange Commission.

formula investing any method of investing that is predetermined and does not vary, regardless of market activity. These include the constant dollar plan and dollar cost averaging.

free and open market a term describing an auction marketplace, in which prices are not controlled. They are allowed to vary based on the level of supply and demand.

front-end load the load fee charged by mutual funds or

sponsors of limited partnerships, which is assessed at the time initial deposits are made.

full disclosure a requirement of the Securities Act of 1933 that all pertinent facts that might affect an investor's decision be disclosed in advance.

fully diluted earnings per share a form of calculating earnings per share, reported as though all convertible securities had been converted to common stock as of the beginning of the year.

fundamental analysis a form of analysis of a corporation including a study of trends in the financial results. This includes tests of financial strength, sales and earnings, dividends paid, and the valuation of assets.

funded debt ratio a ratio that compares working capital to long-term liabilities (consisting of loans and bonds outstanding). The ratio, expressed as a percentage, is the result of subtracting current liabilities from current assets, and dividing the sum by the total funded debt.

futures contract an agreement in which the buyer and seller set a price for the future time and delivery of a commodity.

gross margin ratio a ratio, expressed as a percentage, comparing the gross profit to total sales for a period of time.

gross profit profit earned after deducting direct costs from sales, but before deducting general expenses.

gross sales total sales reported on a company's income statement, without allowing for returns and allowances.

growth stock a stock that, in the opinion of an analyst or investor, holds a high potential for substantial future increases in market value.

head and shoulders chart patterns used in technical analysis, also called *M* or *W* patterns. An *M* pattern is considered a signal that the stock's price will fall, and a *W* pattern indicates that it will rise.

hedge an investing strategy involving the simultaneous purchase and sale of two different but related securities. The strategy limits potential profits and losses.

historical yield a method of calculating earnings in the past, often used to imply likely future profits or to calculate performance of a program or fund.

holder of record the owner of stock as of the date that dividends accrue and are paid.

holding period the duration that an investment is owned.

hypothecation the pledge of securities or cash as collateral, held by the brokerage firm when the client trades on margin.

income statement a financial statement that summarizes the results of operations—sales, direct costs, administrative expenses, income taxes, and net profits or losses—for a period of one year or less.

index fund a mutual fund that invests its portfolio equally in the issues included in an index, so that the overall performance will parallel index movements.

index of leading indicators an index of economic and financial conditions, used to predict market sentiment. Included are oil, auto and steel production rates, employment, the money supply, currency in circulation, personal income, inventories, trade imports and exports, and inflation as measured by the Consumer Price Index.

insider an officer, director, or control person (anyone who owns 10 percent or more of the stock of a corporation) with access to information not yet available to the general public.

insider information news, conditions, or events that are known to insiders but not to the investing public.

institutional investor a mutual fund, insurance company, pension plan, or other large entity that trades in the market for its own account or for the collective accounts of its members. In comparison, individuals are referred to as retail investors.

intangible asset a nonphysical asset; one that does not have tangible value, such as goodwill or the estimated value of covenants, contracts, or rights.

interest 1) the fee charged for borrowing money, or income from lending money to others (paid for bonds and savings accounts, for example);

2) the holding in a security; an open position.

intermediate trend a trend that, according to technicians, precedes a major trend and lasts several weeks or months.

International Association for Financial Planners an association that serves the interests of practitioners in the financial services industry.

internal rate of return the same calculation as **discounted cash flow**; a method of computing return that allows for the time value of money.

inventory turnover a ratio reporting the average number of times an inventory is replaced during the year. The cost of goods sold is divided by average inventory to arrive at the number of turns.

investment adviser a title assumed by individuals offering either advice or the sale of securities.

investment club an organization of usually 15 or fewer individuals who invest as a single unit. This enables the group to share research and analysis and to diversify with a larger pool of capital.

investment company alternate name for a **mutual fund**.

investment goal 1) correctly used, the reason an individual invests. The goal is an intermediate step toward achieving a larger objective. Example: The immediate goals might be to assume moderate risks in a highly liquid investment, to accumulate a larger base of capital, and, eventually, to select other investments;

2) inaccurately used, a description of the attributes of investments, such as income, growth, capital preservation, and liquidity.

investment objective the ultimate purpose of investing, such as to create a fund for retirement or college, to start a new business, or to build an emergency reserve fund. An understanding of the objective dictates the appropriate level of risk, liquidity, and other features in the ideal investment product.

know your customer a standard required by law of all brokers and advisers, as stated in SEC Rule 405. It states that, prior to recommending any investment, the adviser or salesperson must understand the client's risk tolerance, objectives, and preferences.

last sale 1) the final transaction that occurs during a trading day;

2) the price at which the latest sale occurred for a specific security.

legal opinion a letter from an attorney, included in the prospectus, that states an opinion about the issue's compliance with rules and regulations.

leverage the use of money to control additional money, achieved through borrowing. Leverage enables an investor to create a larger base and thus greater potential for future profits. However, because debts must be repaid, leverage also increases risks.

liabilities the debts of a corporation, consisting of accounts and taxes payable, notes, and bonds.

limited partnership an investment in which a number of individuals (limited partners) deposit their funds to purchase units in a program, which are then managed by the general partners.

liquid market a market in which a high volume of trading activity enables many participants to trade without delay.

liquidity 1) a high level of trading volume;
2) the availability of cash, either in accounts or in investments that can be quickly and easily converted to cash.

liquidity ratio an alternate name for the **quick assets ratio**.

load a sales charge, assessed against investors either when cash is deposited (front-end) or when funds are withdrawn (back-end).

locked in a condition of illiquidity, in which the owner of securities cannot sell due to one of three conditions: (1) current value is low and to sell would create a large loss; (2) there is no market for the security; or (3) a long position must be maintained to cover an option written against it.

long the status of an investor's position when he or she owns a security, which is closed by selling it.

long-term assets properties owned by a corporation that are not immediately convertible to cash; capital assets reduced by a reserve for depreciation.

long-term liabilities debts of a corporation that are due and payable beyond the next 12 months.

maintenance requirement a brokerage firm's rules regarding the amount that must be put up as collateral for margin activities.

major trend in technical analysis, the general trend of the market, either bullish or bearish.

margin a method of trading with the use of leverage. An amount of cash or securities is placed with the brokerage firm as collateral, and trading takes place with borrowed funds.

margin of profit the profits of a corporation divided by total sales.

maturity date the date on which the issuer of a bond promises to pay the full face amount.

minor trend in technical analysis, the movement in market prices lasting only a few days, occurring as a deviation away from a major trend.

money market broadly, short-term investments that include federal funds, federal agency bonds, certificates of deposit, banker's acceptances, commercial paper, and short-term municipal bonds. In comparison, long-term debt instruments are collectively called the capital market.

money market fund a mutual fund that invests exclusively in money market instruments.

mutual fund an investment management company that pools the capital of many individuals and diversifies among a group of stocks or bonds, or both. The fund assets are managed by a professional group, within the limitations of a stated investment policy (such as income, aggressive growth, or a balance).

National Association of Investors Corporation (NAIC) a nonprofit association that assists investment clubs with educational and organizational materials, analysis of individual stocks, and regional meetings.

National Association of Securities Dealers (NASD) an agency serving as the self-regulating body of the securities industry. Founded under provisions of the 1938 Maloney Act, the NASD publishes rules of fair practice for member firms and individuals. The agency may fine, censure, or expel members for rule violations.

National Association of Securities Dealers Automated Quotations (NASDAQ) a computerized system used by brokerage firms to find updated quotations for stocks traded over-the-counter and on small exchanges.

National Association of Securities Dealers Automated

Quotations—Over-The-Counter Price Index (NASDAQ–OTC) a broad index that tracks increases and decreases in market value of securities traded over-the-counter.

net asset value per share a calculation used by mutual funds to report on trends in value. It is figured by dividing tangible assets by the number of shares outstanding in the fund.

net book value per share a calculation of book value on a per-share basis, used in fundamental analysis. It is figured by dividing tangible book value by the number of common shares outstanding.

net current assets working capital; the net difference between current assets and current liabilities.

net income ratio the margin of profit; net income divided by sales.

net profit the amount of earnings reported on an income statement, consisting of sales minus cost of goods sold and minus general expenses.

net profit before taxes net profit before deducting an allowance for federal tax liability.

net operating profit profit from activities of the business, not including interest income or expenses, capital gains, foreign exchange gains or losses, and other nonoperational adjustments; and before deducting a provision for federal income tax.

net tangible assets per share a calculation used in fundamental analysis to track the value of a company's common stock. It is figured by reducing total assets by intangibles, liabilities, and the value of preferred stock, and dividing the remainder by the number of common shares outstanding.

net worth the equity of a corporation, the value of stockholder interests; total assets minus total liabilities.

New York Stock Exchange (NYSE) 11 Wall Street, New York, NY 10005. Founded in 1792, the NYSE is the oldest stock exchange in the United States, with listings of most of the largest publicly traded corporations.

no-load a mutual fund or other investment in which no sales fee is charged to investors.

nominal yield the annual yield on a bond, calculated without allowing for semiannual compounding or for premium or discount from face amount.

normal trading unit a round lot; the number of shares or units involved in a trade—for example, 100 shares of stock or blocks divisible by 100.

NYSE Composite Index an index including percentage increases or decreases in value for all stocks traded on the New York Stock Exchange.

odd lot a trade involving fewer than 100 shares of stock.

odd-lot theory in technical analysis, the belief that traders in odd lots are usually wrong about market movements. Thus, increases in odd-lot buying signal the top of the market, and increases in selling signal the bottom.

open-end fund a mutual fund that sells as many shares as the market demands, the most common form of fund. In comparison, a closed-end fund sells a finite number of shares.

option a contract to buy or sell 100 shares of stock, at a fixed price and within a specified period of time. Investors buy or sell options to speculate, to protect (hedge) an opposite position in stock, or to increase total return.

Over-The-Counter (OTC) securities that are traded between brokerage firms rather than on public exchanges.

Pacific Stock Exchange (PSE) 301 Pine Street, San Francisco, CA 94014; a stock exchange second in trading volume only to the New York Stock Exchange, which trades in its own listed securities and those listed on other regional exchanges.

Philadelphia Stock Exchange (PhLX) 1900 Market Street, Philadelphia, PA 10103; an exchange founded in 1790 that engages in stock and option trading.

point and figure chart a chart used in technical analysis, involving the summary of trading range using an x to denote daily increases in price and an o to denote daily decreases.

portfolio the total securities held at any given time by one investor.

preferred stock stock whose owners, in the event of liquidation of the corporation, will be paid before common stockholders. Preferred stock carries no voting rights and, in some classifications, may be converted to common stock.

preliminary prospectus a prospectus given to potential investors in anticipation of a pending final prospectus; also called a **red herring**.

premium 1) the value of a bond in excess of its face amount; 2) the amount paid or received for an option contract.

price/earnings ratio (P/E) a measurement of a stock's demand and popularity, computed by dividing the current market price by the earnings per share for the last 12 months.

price/equity ratio a calculation used in fundamental analysis, figured by dividing current market price by the tangible book value per share of common stock.

prospectus a disclosure document that is given to prospective investors in mutual funds, public limited partnerships, new stock issues, and other programs.

prudent man rule a standard in brokerage and advisory practice, that any advice given to a client must be given with a level of care and diligence.

public offering any offering of securities that is made available to the general public.

qualitative analysis an alternate term for **technical analysis**.

quantitative analysis an alternate term for **fundamental analysis**.

quick assets ratio a calculation used in fundamental analysis to judge the trend in availability of working capital. Current assets less inventories are divided by current liabilities.

quotation the current price of a stock.

rally a surge in overall market prices or, less accurately, in the blue chip issues included on the Dow Jones Industrial Averages.

random walk a theory that no form of analysis can predict the future, since (1) price movement is completely random, and (2) all known facts are already reflected in the current prices of stocks.

range the daily activity of a stock, consisting of the highest, lowest, and closing price.

rate of return the current yield from a security, computed by dividing current income by the basis; also known as return on investment.

Real Estate Investment Trust (REIT) a real estate investment company whose shares trade on public exchanges but whose income is passed through to investors as in a mutual fund.

record date the date on which an investor becomes the owner of stock; the fifth business day following a buy order.

red herring a preliminary prospectus, so called because of the red ink disclosures on the front page.

regional exchanges stock exchanges serving limited geographical areas, including the Boston, Midwest, Intermountain, Spokane, Honolulu, Cincinnati, Detroit, National, Pacific, and Philadelphia exchanges.

Registered Investment Advisor (RIA) an individual or firm offering investment advice and charging a fee.

registered representative an individual who is licensed by the National Association of Securities Dealers (NASD) to execute stock, bond, mutual fund, and limited partnership investment trades.

Regulation T a rule stating the amount that must be kept on deposit with a brokerage firm by customers trading on margin.

resistance level in technical analysis, the highest price that investors are willing to pay for the stock of a company.

retained earnings part of the stockholders' equity of a corporation, represented by profits from previous years that were not paid out in dividends.

return on equity in fundamental analysis, a calculation of the percentage of profit compared to stockholders' equity. It is figured by dividing net income by the total value of net worth.

return on sales a ratio, expressed in percentage form, computed by dividing net profit by sales.

rights the privilege of purchasing additional shares in a company, often at a price below prevailing market price.

risk in its most frequently used connotation, the chance of loss from making an investment. Risk also refers to loss of buying power resulting from inflation, the financial consequences of illiquidity, adverse effects of interest rates, changes in tax legislation, lack of insurance, and unexpected changes in market demand.

round lot a normal trading unit; 100 shares of stock or 10 bonds.

rules of fair practice standards and regulations enacted by the National Association of Securities Dealers (NASD) and imposed on all member organizations and licensed individuals.

safety the degree of protection that, as a feature of any investment, defines the level of risk. An investment that is safe from price deterioration may yield a rate lower than inflation; another may offer a lower degree of safety but have offsetting potential for future profits.

sales charge the load assessed against investors in load mutual funds. The purpose of the load is to compensate the salesperson who placed the business.

secondary movement in technical analysis, a minor trend or temporary deviation from the primary direction of prices.

Securities Act of 1933 law that established the responsibility among brokerage firms and salespeople for full and fair disclosure, including the rule that prospective investors must be given a prospectus.

Securities and Exchange Commission (SEC) the federal agency responsible for regulatory oversight of the securities industry. The SEC was formed as part of the Securities Exchange Act of 1934, and has the power to impose civil fines and to recommend criminal prosecution for violations of law.

Securities Exchange Act of 1934 legislation creating the requirement for licensing of salespeople in the securities industry.

Securities Investor Protection Corporation (SIPC) a non-profit agency of the federal government that insures brokerage accounts placed with member firms.

security 1) an investment for which trading activities are regulated by the SEC;

2) a concept in defining risk and safety, which is that investors desire an acceptable degree of protection from loss. Security is achieved through diversification, insured accounts, minimal or limited chances of loss, and historical performance.

selling climax in technical analysis, a description of trading activity when a stock's price drops dramatically below a previous trading range.

settlement date the date on which buy and sell orders for securities are transferred and must be delivered and paid. For stocks, settlement occurs five business days after the order date.

shareholder the owner of a portion of the stock in a publicly traded corporation.

short the status of holdings when a position has been opened with a sale. The position is closed by a later purchase or, in the case of options, through expiration or exercise.

short interest theory the belief among some technical analysts that trends in short selling predict price movement in the immediate future. As short selling increases, the belief is that the stock's value will rise.

speculation a strategy for pursuing the highest possible return on an investment in the shortest possible time. The speculator is willing to assume a high degree of risk.

split an adjustment in the number of outstanding shares of stock, without changing the overall value. When a stock is split 2 for 1, for example, investors will own twice as many shares as before, but each share will be worth half the value before the split.

Standard & Poor's 500 Index an index that measures market movement based on changes in the prices of 500 industrial, transportation, public utility, and financial stocks.

stockholders' equity the value of equity, or assets minus liabilities, reported on a corporation's balance sheet.

strategy any method used to purchase or sell stocks or to minimize losses. A strategy may involve timing based on technical or fundamental signs.

street name a method for registering securities, in which certificates are registered in the name of the brokerage house on behalf of the client.

suitability a procedure that brokerage firms and salespeople are required to use to determine that an investor meets financial and other standards. Suitability requirements include net worth, available cash, annual income, and the degree of knowledge and experience as an investor.

support level in technical analysis, the lowest price that investors are willing to pay for a stock; for the market as a whole, the lowest price level of an index to which the market is likely to fall.

technical analysis the tracking of prices and trends based on indicators other than financial information. Technicians use charts, indexes, and the measurement of market activity to predict the future.

total return the total yield on an investment that includes allowances for current income as well as increases in market price.

200-day moving average an average used by technical analysts for tracking price movements on the basis of the average price for the last 200 trading days.

unit investment trust a trust that purchases a fixed number of bonds and sells units to investors in the same manner as a closed-end mutual fund. Because the trust has a fixed portfolio, future income and maturity dates are known in advance.

"Value Line Investment Survey" an investment research service that analyzes current fundamental and technical indicators for 1700 common stocks.

vertical line chart a chart summarizing daily price ranges for a stock. The price is tracked from top to bottom, and time is tracked from left to right.

volatility the level of stability or variation in the trading range of a stock. Volatility is measured by dividing the difference between high and low price during the last 12 months by the lowest price, and expressing the result as a percentage.

volume the number of shares traded each day or during a period of time, either for an individual stock or in the market as a whole.

warrant an offer made to investors for the purchase of a limited number of shares at a fixed price. Warrants may or may not have an expiration date, and their value varies with changes in the stock's current market price.

working capital the net of current assets minus current liabilities.

working capital ratio an alternate name for the **current ratio**.

working capital turnover a ratio showing how effectively cash was used to generate income. Net sales are divided by working capital to arrive at the number of turns.

yield the percentage of profit or return on an investment.

yield on common stock the dividend rate, computed by dividing the annual amount paid in dividends by the current market price.

yield to maturity the return an investor will earn if a bond is held to maturity. It includes a calculation of annual interest rate, adjusted by current premium or discount from face value.

APPENDIX

INVESTMENT CLUB PARTNERSHIP AGREEMENT

When you start your investment club, you will need to have each member sign a partnership agreement. It is not necessary to hire an attorney to draw up this document, although you might want your personal attorney to review it before you sign. The laws vary by state; there is a chance that under some circumstances you could be liable for the debts of your partners.

The NAIC recommends using the following partnership agreement:

PARTNERSHIP AGREEMENT

OF THE ___*(name of club)*___

(Names of all partners)

WITNESSETH:

1. Formation of Partnership: The undersigned hereby form a General Partnership, in, and in accordance with the laws of, the state of ___*(your state)*___.

2. Name of Partnership: The name of the partnership shall be ___*(name)*___.

3. Term: The partnership shall begin on ___*(date)*___ and continue until December 31, ___*(year)*___, and thereafter from year to year unless earlier terminated as hereinafter provided.

4. Purpose: The purpose of the partnership is to invest the assets of the partnership solely in stocks, bonds, and securities, for the education and benefit of the partners.

5. Meetings: Periodic meetings shall be held as determined by the partnership.

6. Contributions: The partners may make contributions to the partnership on the date of each periodic meeting, in such amounts as the partnership shall determine, provided, however, that no partner's capital account (as hereinafter defined) shall exceed twenty (20%) per cent of the capital accounts of all partners.

7. Valuation: The current value of the assets of the partnership, less the current value of the debts and liabilities of the partnership, (hereinafter referred to as "value of the partnership") shall be determined as of **10 business** days preceding the date of each periodic meeting. The aforementioned date of valuation shall hereinafter be referred to as "valuation date."

8. Capital Accounts: There shall be maintained in the name of each partner, a capital account. Any increase or decrease in the value of the partnership, on any valuation date shall be credited or debited, respectively, to each partner's capital account in proportion to the value of each partner's capital account on said date. Any other method of valuating each partner's capital account may be substituted for this method provided that said substituted method results in exactly the same valuation as previously provided herein. Each partner's contribution to, or withdrawals from, the partnership shall be credited, or debited, respectively, to that partner's capital account.

9. Management: Each partner shall participate in the management and conduct of the affairs of the partnership in proportion to his capital account. Except as otherwise provided herein, all decisions shall be made by the partners whose capital accounts total a majority in amount of the capital accounts of all the partners.

10. Sharing of Profits and Losses: Net profits and losses of the partnership shall inure to, and be borne by, the partners in proportion to the valuation adjusted credit balances in their capital accounts or in proportion to valuation unit balances.

11. Books of Account: Books of account of the transactions of the partnership shall be kept and at all times be available and open to inspection and examination by any partner.

12. Annual Accounting: Each calendar year, a full and complete account of the condition of the partnership shall be made to the partners.

13. Bank Account: The partnership shall select a bank for the purpose of opening a partnership bank account. Funds deposited in said partnership bank account shall be withdrawn by check signed by either of two (2) partners designated by the partnership.

14. Broker Account: None of the partners of this partnership shall be a broker; however, the partnership may select a broker and enter into such agreements with the broker as required, for the purchase or sale of stocks, bonds and securities. Stocks, bonds and other securities owned by the partnership shall be registered in the partnership name unless another name shall be designated by the partnership.

Any corporation or Transfer Agent called upon to transfer any stocks, bonds and securities to or from the name of the partnership shall be entitled to rely upon instructions or assignments signed or purporting to be signed by any partner without inquiry as to the authority of the persons signing or purporting to sign such instructions or assignments or as to the validity of any transfer to or from the name of the partnership.

At the time of transfer, the corporation or transfer agent is entitled to assume (1) that the partnership is still in existence and (2) that this agreement is in full force and effect and has not been amended unless the corporation has received written notice to the contrary.

15. No Compensation: No partner shall be compensated for services rendered to the partnership, except reimbursement for expenses.

16. Additional Partners: Additional partners may be admitted at any time, upon the unanimous consent of all the partners in writing or at a meeting so long as the number of partners does not exceed fifteen.

17. Voluntary Termination: The partnership may be dissolved by agreement of the partners whose capital accounts total a majority in amount of the capital accounts of all the partners. Notice of said decision to dissolve the partnership shall be given to all the partners. The partnership shall thereupon be terminated by the payment of all the debts and liabilities of the partnership and the distribution of the remaining assets either in cash or in kind, to the partners or their personal representatives in proportion to their capital valuation accounts.

18. Withdrawal of a Partner: Any partner may withdraw a part or all of his interest. He shall give notice in writing to the recording partner. His notice shall be deemed to be received as of the first meeting of the club at which it is presented. If notice is received between meetings, it will be treated as received at the first following meeting. In making payment the valuation statement prepared for the first meeting following the meeting at which notice is received will be used to determine the value of the partner's account. Between receipt of notice and the withdrawal valuation date, the other partners shall have and are given the option during said period to purchase, in proportion to their capital accounts in the partnership, the capital account of the withdrawing partner. If the other partners do not exercise their option to purchase, then the partnership shall pay the withdrawing partner the value of his interest in the partnership as shown by the valuation statement in accordance with paragraph 20 of this partnership agreement.

19. Death or Incapacity of a Partner: In the event of the death or incapacity of a partner, receipt of such notice shall be treated as a notice of withdrawal. Liquidation and payment of the partner's account shall proceed in accordance with paragraphs 18 and 20.

20. Purchase Price: Upon the death, incapacity or withdrawal of a partner, and the exercise of the option to purchase by the other partners, said other partners shall pay the withdrawing partner or his estate, as the case may be, a purchase price, when payment is made in cash, equal to ninety-seven per cent of his capital account or his capital account less the actual cost of selling sufficient securities to obtain the cash to meet the withdrawal, whichever is the lesser amount. Said purchase price shall be paid within two weeks after the valuation date used in determining the purchase price. In the case of a complete withdrawal in liquidation of a partner's entire interest, payment may be made in cash or securities at the option of the remaining partners of the club. In the case of a partial withdrawal in partial liquidation of a partner's interest, payment may be made in cash or securities at the option of the withdrawing partner. Where payment is made in securities, the full purchase price of the account will be paid the partner for that part of the account purchased with securities. If the partner desires an advance payment, the club at its earliest convenience may pay him 80% of the estimated value of his account and settle the balance of the account in accordance with the valuation date set in paragraph 18. Where payment is made in securities, the club's broker shall be advised that the ownership of the securities has been changed at least by the valuation date used for the withdrawal.

21. Forbidden Acts: No partner shall:

> *(a)* Have the right or authority to bind or obligate the partnership to any extent whatsoever with regard to any matter outside the scope of the partnership's business.

(b) Without the unanimous consent of all the other partners, assign, transfer, pledge, mortgage or sell all or part of his interest in the partnership to any other partner or other person whomsoever, or enter into any agreement as the result of which any person or persons not a partner shall become interested with him in the partnership.

(c) Purchase an investment for the partnership where less than the full purchase price is paid for same.

(d) Use the partnership name, credit or property for other than partnership purposes.

(e) Do any act detrimental to the interests of the partnership or which would make it impossible to carry on the business or affairs of the partnership.

This Agreement of Partnership is hereby declared and shall be binding upon the respective heirs, executors, administrators and personal representatives of the parties.

IN WITNESS WHEREOF, the parties have set their hands and seals the year and day first above written.

Partners:

(Signatures of partners)

_____

(Reprinted with permission from *The Investors Manual*, published by the National Association of Investors Corporation, 1515 Eleven Mile Road, Royal Oak MI 48067)

INDEX

AAII Journal, 126
Accounting methods, 68
Advance–decline line, 34
Alternative investments, 5
American Association of Individual
    Investors:
  membership benefits, 125–126
  seminars, 126–127
  software resources, 57
American College, 149
American Stock Exchange Price
    Change Index, 31
Annual report:
  auditor's letter, 64–67
  financial statements, 72–76
  footnotes, 70–71
  manipulation, 67–70
  statement analysis, 76–82
  supplements to, 83–84
Assets
  buying and selling, 68
  current, 74
  intangible, 74
  long-term, 74
  valuation, 71
Auditor's letter, 64–67
Automated research, 56–57

Back-end load, 96
Balance sheet, 72, 73
Banking earnings, 67
Barron's Confidence Index, 35
Barron's National Business and
    Financial Weekly, 115–116

Beta, 37
Better Investing, 57
Block trading, 36
Boardroom Reports, 126
Book value per share, 25
Borrowings, 70
Bottom Line, 126
Breadth of the market, 33
Breakaway gap, 40
Breakout pattern, 40, 42
Broker research, 48–51
Broker and financial planner:
  and plan development, 156–160
  and safety, 155–156
  certification, 148–149
  commissions, 151
  discounting, 154–155
  fees, 152–153
  perspectives, 150–153
  registration, 148
  working with, 160–161
Business Week, 118, 126
Buying assets, 68

Certified financial planner, 148
Certified public accountant, 149
Changes in stockholders' equity,
    72–73
Changing Times, 119
Charles Schwab & Company, 57
Chart:
  breakout, 40, 42
  climax, 42, 44
  deviation, 40

203

204 Index

Chart *(cont.)*
  double signals, 40, 42, 43
  head and shoulders, 40, 41
  point and figure, 38–39
  predictability, 40
  resistance levels, 40
  support levels, 40
  vertical line, 39
Chartered financial consultant, 148–149
Climax pattern, 42, 44
College for Financial Planning, 148
Commodity Futures Trading Commission, 58
CompuServe Information Services, 56
Computerized Investing, 126
Confidence index, 35
Consumer Information Center, 58
Contingent liabilities, 71
Contrarian theory, 31
Cost estimates, 68
Cost of goods sold, 75–76
Costs and expenses, 68
Current assets and liabilities, 74
Current ratio, 77–78

Debt/equity ratio, 81
Deferred sales charge, 96
Deviation of price, 40
Disclosure problems, 86–87
Dividends, 24
Double signals, 40, 42, 43
Dow Jones & Company, 57
Dow Jones Industrial Averages, 30–31
Dow Jones News/Retrieval, 56
Dow Theory, 29
"Dow Theory Forecasts," 108

Earnings per share, 25–26
Earnings per share ranking, 116
Efficient market theory, 27–28
8-K, 84
Equally weighted index, 31
Excessive leverage, 11–12, 13

Exit fee, 96
Expenses, 76
Expertise, 59–60

Federal income taxes, 76
Federal Reserve System, 58
Financial newspaper:
  advantages, 114
  and magazines, 118–119
  applications, 119–121
  information sources, 114–118
  timing, 121–124
Financial plan, 156–160
Financial statements, 24
Financial World, 118
Footnotes, 70–71
Forbes, 118, 126
Fortune, 118, 126
Free seminars, 127–130
Front-end load, 96
Fundamental analysis:
  and book value, 25
  defined, 20
  dividend, 24
  earnings, 25–26
  financial statement, 24
  price, 26
  trends, 23

Goals, 2–4
"Granville Market Letter," 108
Gross profit, 76
Gross sales, 75
"Growth Stock Outlook," 102, 108

Head and shoulders pattern, 40, 41
Hidden fees, 94–98
Hulbert Financial Digest, 107–108

Illiquidity, 9–10, 13
Income statement, 72, 75
Independent research, 51–56
Industry trends, 37
Inflation, 10, 13
Insider trading, 32
Insurance risk, 11, 13

Intangible assets, 74
International Association for Financial Planning, 149
Inventory turnover ratio, 79–80
Investment:
 alternatives, 5
 classes, 130–132
 losses, 9
 matching, 15–17
 nonsecurity, 59–61
 standards, 4–5, 165–168
Investment advisory letter:
 credentials, 108–110
 predictions, 101–108
Investment club:
 formation, 142–145
 goals, 141–142
 partnership agreement, 197–202
 statistics, 140–141
 values, 137–139
Investment Company Institute, 58
Investment Management Consultants Association, 149
Investment tracking:
 evaluation, 172–174
 records, 168–170
 standards, 165–168
 trades, 170–172
Investor confidence, 35
Investor's Daily, 116–118, 120
Investor's Guide to No-Load Mutual Funds, 126

Leverage, 11–12, 13
Liabilities, 74
Limited partnership prospectus, 90–94
Load, 95, 98
Long-term assets and liabilities, 74
Losses, 9

Management fees, 95
Manipulation of profits, 67–70
Market Analyzer, 57
"Market Briefs," 101–102
"Market Logic," 108

Market Manager Plus, 57
Matching investments, 15–17
Microcomputer Resource Guide, 57
Money, 119
Moving average, 28, 29
Mutual fund:
 indicators, 32
 prospectus, 87–90
"Mutual Fund Values," 57–58

National Association of Investors Corporation:
 membership, 140–141
 software resources, 57
National Association of Securities Dealers, 148
National Association of Securities Dealers Automated Quotations—Over-the-Counter Price Index, 31
Net operating profit, 76
Net profit, 76
New issues, 36–37
New York Stock Exchange Index, 31
No-load, 95, 98
Nonsecurity investments, 59–61
North American Securities Administrators Association, 147

Odd-lot index, 33
Other income/expenses, 76
"The Outlook," 55–56, 105, 108

Partnership agreement, 197–202
Point and figure chart, 38–39
Portfolio tracking record, 169
Predictability of price, 40
Prediction techniques, 103–108
Preliminary prospectus, 85
Price/earnings ratio, 26
Price-weighted index, 31
Primary movement, 29
"Professional Tape Reader," 108
Prospectus:
 and informed decisions, 98–99
 disclosure problems, 86–87

206   Index

Prospectus *(cont.)*
  hidden fees, 94–98
  limited partnership, 90–94
  mutual fund, 87–90
Protecting interests, 61–62
Public marketplace, 59

Quick assets ratio, 78

Ratio:
  current, 77–78
  debt/equity, 81
  inventory turnover, 79–80
  price/earnings, 26
  quick assets, 78
  return on sales, 82
  working capital turnover, 80–81
Red herring, 85
Registered investment adviser, 149
Registered representative, 148
Registry of Financial Planning
    Practitioners, 149
Relative price strength, 116
Research, 5, 7–15, 48–59
Resistance level, 40
Return on sales, 82
Risk:
  illiquidity, 9–10, 13
  inflation, 10, 13
  insurance, 11, 13
  leverage, 11–12, 13
  loss, 9
  tax, 10–11, 13

Safety ranking, 52–54
Sales load, 95
SchwabQuotes, 57
SEC Rule 430, 85
Secondary movement, 29
Securities Act of 1933, 85
Securities and Exchange
    Commission, 83
Select Information Exchange,
    109–110
Self-interest of dealers, 60
Selling assets, 68

Seminars and classes:
  AAII, 126–127
  free, 127–130
  investment, 130–132
  membership, 125–127
Short interest, 35
Significant accounting policies, 70
Standard & Poor's:
  Corporation, 55–56
  500 Index, 31
  track record, 105
Standards for investing, 4–5
Statement of changes in financial
    position, 72
Stock options, 71
Stockholders' equity, 74
Stock selection worksheet, 166–167
Support levels, 40
Sylvia Porter's Personal Finance,
    119

Tax risk, 10–11, 13
Technical analysis:
  advance–decline line, 34
  beta, 37
  block trading, 36
  breadth of the market, 33
  charting, 38–45
  defined, 21
  indexes, 30–31
  indicators, 31–38
  industry trend, 37
  insider trading, 32
  investor confidence, 35
  mutual fund, 32
  new issue, 36–37
  odd-lot index, 33
  short interest, 35
  volatility, 37–38
  volume, 35–36
"Telephone Switch Newsletter," 108
10-K, 83–84
10-Q, 83–84
Timeliness ranking, 52–54
Timing, 68
Trading summary, 171

Trends, 23, 28
12b-1 fee, 96–97

"United Business Service," 108
Unusual items, 70–71

Valuation of assets, 71
Value Line:
  index, 31
  Investment Survey, 52–56
  track record, 104–105, 108
Vertical line chart, 39

Volatility, 37–38
Volume, 35–36
Volume percentage change, 116–118

Wall Street Journal, 114–116
Warrants, 71
Working capital turnover ratio, 80–81

Year-End Tax Strategy Guide, 126

"Zweig Forecast," 108